"With a wicked wit and expansive erudition, Abraham Socher's collected essays—written, as he says, 'while playing hooky' from academic research—add up to much more than the half-dozen scholarly books that he might have written on the job. Whether pondering the meaning of death in the Kaddish, dissecting a series of ugly incidents at Oberlin College, or riffing on American popular culture, Socher offers succinct and bracing wisdom for our contentious times. Taken together, *Liberal and Illiberal Arts* establishes Socher as a master of the art of the essay." —**David Biale**, Emanuel Ringelblum Distinguished Professor of Jewish History, University of California, Davis, and author of *Gershom Scholem: Master of the Kabbalah*

"*Liberal and Illiberal Arts* is at once both dazzling and engaging." —**David Ellenson**, Chancellor Emeritus of Hebrew Union College-Jewish Institute of Religion, and author of *Jewish Meaning in a World of Choice*

"In an era where our intellectual life is muddy with ideology, our religious life muddy with politics, our political life muddy with moral posturing, and our morality muddy with self-righteousness, Socher performs an enormous public service and clears away the mud. In this moving collection, he offers us what we direly need: clarity." —**Dara Horn**, author of *People Love Dead Jews*

"What has Los Angeles to do with Jerusalem? More than you might think, Abraham Socher shows in these wonderfully learned and inviting essays. Here Bogart and Maimonides, baseball's steroids scandal and a raucous party at a 19th-century yeshiva, Nabokov's *Pale Fire* and the Kaddish prayer, all mingle happily, brought together by Socher's love of intellectual exploration. Plenty of books have been written in defense of the idea of the liberal arts, but this one is a living example of their power to charm and enlighten."

of *The Blessing and the Curse: The Jew the Twentieth Century*

"Abraham Socher is that rare writer who combines a light touch with vast learning and deep insight. On matters as ostensibly diverse as classical Jewish thought, the history of baseball, the relationship of philosophy to religion, and the groupthink currently undermining colleges and universities, he has valuable things to say and says them in a delightful style, leavened by subtle wit." —**Jon D. Levenson**, Albert A. List Professor of Jewish Studies, Harvard Divinity School, and author of *The Love of God: Divine Gift, Human Gratitude, and Mutual Faithfulness in Judaism*

"With his insatiable curiosity, eye for the killer detail, and frame of reference wide as the diaspora, Abraham Socher is an essayist for the ages. These gems remind us what the rabbis meant by learn: to inquire as deeply of texts as one does of life, death, and love." —**Esther Schor**, Leonard L. Milberg '53 Professor of American Jewish Studies, Princeton University, and author of *Bridge of Words: Esperanto and the Dream of a Universal Language*

"Socher has an enviable command of Jewish texts, ancient, modern, esoteric, and popular. But he's not just a scholar. He's a magician. In these lovely, lucid essays, Socher turns his considerable erudition into deceptively plain prose. Encountering cant and contradiction, he politely slices them asunder. We who care about Jewish ideas and letters are lucky to have a Socher to keep them honest and intelligible." —**Judith Shulevitz**, author of *The Sabbath World*

"Few master the complexities of contemporary culture as deftly as Abraham Socher, whose breadth of knowledge never fails to astonish. To all that he touches, he brings an uncommon blend of erudition, wit, and moral engagement." —**Steven J. Zipperstein**, Daniel E. Koshland Professor in Jewish Culture and History, Stanford University, and author of *Pogrom: Kishinev and the Tilt of History*

Liberal and Illiberal Arts

LIBERAL

AND

ILLIBERAL
ARTS

Essays

(MOSTLY JEWISH)

ABRAHAM SOCHER

PAUL DRY BOOKS
Philadelphia 2022

First Paul Dry Books edition, 2022

Paul Dry Books, Inc.
Philadelphia, Pennsylvania
www.pauldrybooks.com

Copyright © 2022 Abraham Socher
All rights reserved

ISBN-13: 978-1-58988-160-0

Printed in the United States of America

Library of Congress Control Number: 2021952879

For Shoshana

Contents

III. LIFE AND AFTERLIFE

Liberal and Illiberal Arts

Introduction

A LITTLE OVER twenty years ago, I interviewed to be an assistant professor of Jewish history at a big state university, which I'll call the U of A. After giving a job talk about the quirky philosopher-heretic Solomon Maimon, in which I tried to impress a skeptical just-the-facts-ma'am historian with my command of the demography of eighteenth-century East European Jewry, I was taken to meet an associate dean (big building, small office, blue blazer).

The dean, who was a scientist of some kind, asked me if I enjoyed teaching. I leapt into an enthusiastic, largely sincere bit about the first-year humanities courses I was teaching as a post-doc at Stanford that year. Two or three sentences in, the dean waved me off. "Oh, I don't care," he said, "it's just something I'm required by the state legislature to ask you. We're an R-1 university. You'll live and die here based on your *research*: for tenure, you'll need several articles in peer-reviewed journals in your subfield—you guys do have those, don't you?—a book with an excellent university press and maybe another one on the way, or at least an active research agenda."

Although I'd never before heard the term "R-1 university" (perhaps because the schools I had attended thought that they were tiers unto themselves), I knew the rest. Still, the bluff, bureaucratic good humor with which this dean of arts and sciences dismissed the importance of how I would teach shortly before offering me a job as a teacher was startling. Also, I'd never quite thought of what I actually did—browsing in the library stacks, making fortuitous connections, thinking hard about a literary passage or philosophical argument—as research, exactly. Sitting in the dean's office with my careerist academic game face on, I suddenly realized that he didn't really care what research in the history of Jewish philosophy, or the philosophy of Jewish history, or whatever it was that I did, amounted to. All that mattered was that there was a way to quantify it—and a tenure line in his budget. (The fact that this line was probably funded by a donor less concerned about Jewish history than about the Jewish future of U of A undergraduates was something to which neither the dean nor I gave a second thought.)

In the end, I took a position at Oberlin College instead. They had more or less the same tenure requirements, but, to their credit, the Oberlin faculty and dean made it clear to me that I would also have to become an excellent teacher. More importantly, the students—bright, curious, questing—made it even clearer that they would make me ashamed of myself if I didn't. They were, many of them anyway, interested in knowledge for its own sake, though they also were encouraged to think that it would end up coinciding with personal, political, and perhaps even spiritual virtue. Indeed, that dubious equation was literally Oberlin's selling point ("Think one person can save the world? So do we," read the admissions tagline).

Although I'd spent all but a year or so of my life on campuses since I was seventeen, I'd never been at a liberal arts

college. The idea of a school that put undergraduate curiosity at the center of its intellectual life was thrilling to me.
Later, I would realize that there are threats to the liberal
arts at Oberlin at least as stultifying as the big-university
scientism at U of A, and they started with that illiberal
equation between knowledge and virtue. But that is getting
ahead of myself.

Some of these essays grew out of lectures I gave at Oberlin—or, more precisely, digressions from those lectures.
But mostly I wrote them while I was playing hooky. I'd be
sitting in my office with a stack of bluebooks to grade, or
in the library working on a conference paper, when some
almost stray historical fancy or textual puzzle would seize
me. For instance, how did Humphrey Bogart end up telling a semi-Platonic midrash about babies, knowledge, and
facial anatomy to Lauren Bacall in *Key Largo*? Just what
poetic "pale fire" had Nabokov stolen from Robert Frost?
Or, did the preeminent Talmudic scholar Saul Lieberman
really introduce Gershom Scholem, his opposite number in
the study of Jewish mysticism, with the quip "nonsense is
nonsense but the history of nonsense is a very important
science"? (Lieberman's joke is, I now realize, more or less
what that dean at U of A thought about research into my
particular art or science—to the extent that he thought
about it at all.)

Once I had one of these whimsical bits between my teeth,
I'd be off to the races and no good to anyone until the question had become an essay. That is to say, not an article in
a peer-reviewed journal, but rather something between an
argument and a story that aimed to entertain and edify
without nailing any theses to the wall. Some of these essays,
such as the three mentioned above, touch on big, general
questions: How does a myth make itself at home in a new
culture—and how do people (Jews, for instance)? What's
the deep connection between allusion and literary inspi-

ration? Does the modern disenchanted study of religion inevitably disenchant religion itself? But, in most cases, I hope that they only *touch* on such questions. For how many of us can do more than that, and how much more is there really to do? I'd rather find the small human story behind a great or favorite book than use it to propound or confirm a big theory.

Sometimes, when I was teaching, an earnest student would want to know why we were focusing on, say, a particular image in the work of Spinoza, or the intricacies of a Talmudic argument about ownership, rather than the Cosmos itself or Justice writ large. I usually replied by saying something about the importance of getting the details right or making a remark about the part and the whole, but often I would also think of a few lines in Nabokov's "Evening of Russian Poetry." The visiting speaker is going on about how the Cyrillic alphabet has taken on aspects of the Russian landscape, when he is interrupted:

> Yes, Sylvia?
>   *"Why do you speak of words*
>   *when all we want is knowledge nicely browned?"*

This desire for the neat moral, the nicely browned nugget, a socio-political message easily detachable from its particular context, is one of the enemies of a liberal education, and not only at left-wing liberal artsy schools like Oberlin. The conservative approach can yield its own generalizations nicely browned into meaninglessness; Mortimer Adler, the University of Chicago's great books czar, once listed 102 of them in his sublimely boring *Synopticon*. (Nabokov's answer to Sylvia begins: "Because all hangs together—shape and sound,/heather and honey, vessel and content./Not only rainbows—every line is bent. . . .")

Of course, I wasn't always mooning over the subtle allusions and witticisms of my mid-century culture heroes while avoiding grading midterms or writing my upcoming lecture. Sometimes I was reviewing a book (some late stories of Ozick, a life of Bellow or the Lubavitcher Rebbe, Senator Mitchell's report on steroids in baseball), and sometimes I was reviewing my own life with the help of books (those of Maimonides, Montaigne, and the Mussarniks, among others), which wasn't R-1 research, but wasn't exactly playing hooky either.

In fact, about thirteen years ago, three things happened that changed how I wrote, both vessel and content. Our youngest daughter, Bayla, was born and immediately underwent a successful open heart surgery (and then a second one), my father died rather suddenly, and I started a magazine called the *Jewish Review of Books*. The result was that I found myself thinking a lot about human fragility and death, but I had also somehow managed to turn playing hooky, at least my kind of hooky, into a profession, though for several years I didn't give up my day job as a professor.

I GREW UP bouncing back and forth between private Jewish day schools and public schools. This was partly about money and partly about my family feeling as American as we felt Jewish. For high school, however, I ended up in a yeshiva in the San Fernando Valley that tried to recreate not only the scholarly and religious ethos of its mother school in New York, but even that of its more distant predecessors in Lithuania. Although I hesitate to count the number of years of formal schooling I underwent after graduating from this yeshiva high school, my conception of what it was to study, or, as we were to taught to say, to *learn* was formed there.

The yeshiva's building had been repurposed from some earlier hard-to-guess institutional use—a clinic? an orphanage? one of those sinister LA sanitariums from a Raymond Chandler novel?—and the whole school had a ramshackle, provisional air. As a student, one had the sense that everything, or almost everything, was up for negotiation with the rabbis who ran the place, and that the secular teaching staff wasn't in on the real deal. It was like a family business where the unrelated employees imagine that there are uniform official policies. Everything was up for negotiation because precisely one thing wasn't: the study of Torah, which largely meant Talmud, was non-negotiable. The idea that there was nothing more important than the absurdly close study of ancient texts about seemingly obscure matters of ritual and civil law, and that this study should be pursued for its own sake (*Torah lishmah*), was enormously exciting to me then, and still is.

At the time, I thought that the rosh yeshiva, into whose class I quickly managed to get myself promoted, was a genius. I now see that he was, rather, teaching—or, one might say, channeling—a tradition of genius, though that too is a great achievement. In this case, it was not just the rabbinic tradition in general but that tradition as it flowed through Slabodka and Radin to Forest Hills in Queens and, improbably, into "the Valley."

I remember sitting in the rosh yeshiva's *shiur* trying to keep four or five levels of legal interpretation clear in my head, while looking out the window behind him, through the smudged glass and broken security screens overtaken by browning foliage, past the basketball court and the cinderblock wall and into the blue LA sky, when the two experiences, sensory and intellectual, seemed suddenly to merge. Later, it occurred to me that there is a famous teaching in *Chapters of the Fathers*: that "one who is walking on the road studying, and interrupts his study to say 'that tree

is so beautiful' or 'that field is so beautiful'" has committed a mortal sin. But that synesthetic moment stays with
me even now: the sense of an intellectual tradition that was
infinite, or nearly so, and the way in which the beauty of
a text, a thought really, was both unlike the beauty of the
world and a part of it.

Such epiphanies, however, did not keep me from playing
hooky. About half a mile down Laurel Canyon Boulevard
from my high school was Dutton's Books and Fine Prints,
which, though it sat unpromisingly between a gas station
and a Kentucky Fried Chicken outlet, was one of the best
bookstores in Los Angeles. Sometimes I'd slip out of school
on a warm Valley afternoon (the dual religious-secular
curriculum meant that the school day went on forever),
and walk down to Dutton's and browse its tightly packed
shelves, overflowing tables, and book-crowded nooks of
forbidden secular literature.

If this were a just-so autobiographical story, I would tell
you that I used to go to the fiction shelves at the back of
Dutton's and read Bellow and Nabokov, and that, years
later, I picked up a copy of Peter Berger's *Sacred Canopy* in
the social science alcove: so, some of these essays of my
middle age actually began with my playing hooky in high
school. But sometimes life is just so, and that's how it happened, more or less. Although I didn't know it at the time,
one of the Duttons, Denis, was a philosopher who founded
a great aggregator website in the 1990s called Arts & Letters Daily, which linked snappy book reviews and serious
essays. When I found this out, I wrote Dutton and thanked
him and his family for the years of physical and virtual
browsing. Still later, when I first published some of the
essays in this book, including the ones on Bellow and Peter
Berger, they were linked on Arts & Letters Daily, though
by then the website was operated by *The Chronicle of Higher
Education*, and Dutton had passed away.

The essays collected here were written over the last eighteen years. I've arranged them in a loose thematic order, which does not segregate the handful of "non-Jewish" essays from the Jewish ones. In the first place, my way of writing and thinking is no different when discussing Nabokov and Frost or steroids in baseball than it is when discussing, say, Gershom Scholem's kabbalistic hopes for Walter Benjamin or a raucous synagogue party in Boisk. In the second, sometimes such lines are hard to draw. For instance, "Is Repentance Possible?" is the essay here that comes closest to being a *derashah* (sermon) of sorts, but it spends as much time with Alasdair MacIntyre as it does with Maimonides. Conversely, my discussion of Don DeLillo's novel about cryogenics segues into rabbinic ideas about resurrection of the dead. In short, even when these essays take on current books or perennial issues, they are personal and so follow my own interests back and forth across that porous border.

I am fortunate to have been born during a period when it has been possible—or at least has seemed so—to lead a life that is both wholly Jewish and unapologetically American (or the other way around). But the melting pot continues to bubble, and this somewhat golden age, which stretched from mid-century to the day before yesterday, probably won't last another lifetime. The implications of this sociological fact is a concern of several essays in the collection, especially in the first part of the book.

The second part of the book is largely devoted to twentieth-century Jewish intellectuals, their sayings and doings. This is mostly a chronicle of heroes, men and women devoted to thinking deeply and writing well—those whose books and essays partly constitute at least one version of a liberal education. But there are some illiberal villains to be found as well, particularly in the chapter, the longest in the book, that tells the story of a disgraceful incident at Oberlin College, where I began my career in the liberal arts some two decades ago.

My daughter's difficult birth and my father's passing not long after brought home to me what it means to care for someone in their vulnerability, which, it turns out, is what it means to care for someone at all. I begin this collection with an essay about a perhaps-Platonic Jewish folktale about knowledge and birth, so it may seem a little too perfect, a little too "on the nose," as we now say, to end it with essays about fragility, death, and the idea of an afterlife. On the other hand, death is almost always behind our sense of an ending, as it is also behind our desire for eternity. As it says in the Mourner's Kaddish, which I discuss in the final essay, "May His great name be praised forever and for all time."

I

Blank Tablets

AND

Bad Hebrew Schools

How the Baby Got Its Philtrum

SOMETIME AFTER World War II, Humphrey Bogart, or rather Frank McCloud, goes out to the Florida Keys to visit the father (Lionel Barrymore) and young widow (Lauren Bacall) of a soldier named George Temple who had been under his command in the Battle of San Pietro. The soldier's father asks McCloud to tell him something about how his son died.

McCloud: Three days and three nights he stayed awake directing our fire. Most of that time I was on the other end of the line. To keep himself awake, he talked into the phone. Talked and talked . . . Most of his talk was about you two. You'd be surprised how much I know about you both. For instance, inside your wedding ring there's an inscription: "Evermore."

Nora Temple: That's right.

Frank McCloud: And you, Mr. Temple. Remember telling George what this hollow is above the upper lip? Before he was born, you said, he knew all the secrets of life and death. And then at his birth, an angel came and put his finger right here [touching his upper lip] and sealed his lips.

James Temple: I remember that! Yep. He couldn't have been more than seven years old when I told him that fairy story.

I've wondered on and off over the years just how this Jewish legend ended up on Bogart's lips. *Key Largo* (1948) is based on Maxwell Anderson's play of the same name, but Anderson was the son of a Baptist minister, and, as far as I know, there is no Christian version of this just-so "fairy story" of how the baby got its philtrum—which is the name of that little, centered hollow we all have above our lips. It also doesn't sound like Anderson. I was reminded of this and related mysteries recently while gazing at my newest granddaughter, a gray-eyed infant who gazed back with a somber, seemingly knowing look.

As it turns out, there isn't much of a mystery as to how Anderson got ahold of the story: He didn't. John Huston, the film's director, hated Anderson's play—"That son of a bitch, he can't write!"—and worked with a young screenwriter named Richard Brooks to rewrite it from scratch. And Brooks was born Reuben Sax, to Russian-Jewish immigrants, so I'd be willing to bet that he is the source of this little bit of mythological stage business. But there is, it turns out, a mystery as to the origin of the myth itself.

Over the last few weeks, I've asked a couple of dozen Jews—men and women, scholars and laypeople, raised in homes ranging from secular to Orthodox—whether they heard this story growing up. Most of them had. The literary scholar Howard Schwartz recently retold it in a children's book called *Before You Were Born*. Schwartz, like seemingly everyone else who has thought about it, traces the story to a famous Talmudic discussion of the embryo and soul before birth and its further elaborations in later rabbinic literature, but that's not quite right.

Rabbi Simlai, a Talmudic preacher famous for saying that there are precisely 613 commandments in the Torah, taught that the embryo sits in its mother's womb like "folded writing tablets, its hands rest on its two temples, its two elbows on its two legs, and its heels against its behind."

There is no time in which a man enjoys greater happiness than in those days, as it is said, "O that I were as in months gone by, in the days when God watched over me, when his lamp shone over my head, when I walked in the dark by its light" (Job 29:2,3) . . . [these are] the months of pregnancy. It is also taught the entire Torah . . . and it says "God's company graced my tent" (Job 29:4). As soon as it sees the light, an angel comes and slaps it on the mouth and it forgets the entire Torah (Niddah, 30b).

An early medieval text, *Midrash Tanhuma*, adds several colorful details, including that the angel's name is Laila (Night), but it is still a slap on the mouth, not a mythic caress on the upper lip, nor does it explain the little indent beneath one's septum.

If Rabbi Simlai's myth explains any physiological mystery, it is, as a contemporary Israeli Yemenite rabbinic authority Rabbi Yitzhaq Ratzabi has pointed out, how the baby chooses a particular moment to enter the world and why it cries when it does. Ratzabi knows the legend of the philtrum, but dismisses it as having no Talmudic basis. Rabbi Chaim Kanievsky, the current reigning Ashkenazi authority among Israeli *haredim*, has been quoted to similar effect. Nonetheless, they both know the legend and neither of them got it from Humphrey Bogart on Amazon Prime Video.

The philosophical point that seems to hover over this Talmudic passage and its later elaborations is that learning is really an act of recall. As Rabbi Joseph Soloveitchik once wrote, "Rabbi Simlai wanted to tell us that when a Jew studies Torah, he is confronted with something . . . familiar, because he has already studied it and the knowledge was stored up in the recesses of his memory." As Soloveitchik and others, including the nineteenth-century scholar Adolph Jellinek, who published an elaborate medieval version of the tale, recognized, this seems to be a version of Plato's famous theory of knowledge as recollection. However, it's worth noting that although these texts speak of the unborn child as forgetting, they don't explicitly describe its later learning as an act of recovery through memory.

The Maharal of Prague came close when he suggested that the angel slaps the unborn child's mouth to create "a lack and a desire," by which he seems to have meant both a desire to nurse and a desire to learn. But the Maharal lived in sixteenth-century Prague when Plato was, once again, on every intellectual's lips. It wasn't until some 200 years later that Rabbi Elimelekh of Lizhensk explicitly argued that if we hadn't learned Torah before we entered the world it would be impossible to grasp it now—call that a Hasidic footnote to Plato.

Certainly, the idea of learning as a recovery of what we once possessed is what makes Bogart's *bubbe mayse*, and ours, so memorable: We can all touch that little hollow and feel the impress of forgotten knowledge. But—to repeat the question you may have forgotten amidst the flurry of sources—when did the angel's slap become a gentle, indenting touch?

It may have been faintly suggested by a reading of the *Zohar*'s parallel discussion, in which the angel marks or presses, rather than slaps, the fetus on the mouth before it is born (the verb is *roshem*), but the medieval classic of Jewish mysticism doesn't say anything about philtrums. Several hundred years later, Rabbi Schneur Zalman of Liadi, the founder of Chabad Hasidism (and Rabbi Elimelekh's younger contemporary), still thought of the angel's touch as closer to the Talmudic slap than a gentle touch. We know this from a story Martin Buber retells about his refusal to move back in with his mother-in-law. Having finally recognized his spiritual greatness, she wanted to make up for how she and her husband had treated him in the early years of his marriage to their daughter, so she invited her son-in-law and daughter to move back into their house. The Alter Rebbe refused. "Look," he, said, "Who can be better off than the child in its mother's womb? He need not . . . worry about his food and his drink, and all day he learns the entire Torah. But when the child is born, an angel comes and strikes him on the mouth, and he forgets all that he has learned. And yet—even if he were able to return, he would not want to. . . . Because he has reached his full measure."

So, when did the actual legend of the baby's hollow appear? Who created the origin story that screenwriter Richard Brooks put into Bogart's mouth? Brooks probably heard the story himself when he was, like his character, not "more than seven years old," which would be around 1920, a few years before Rabbi Kanievsky would have heard it in Pinsk and a few decades before Rabbi Ratzabi would have done so in Kfar Saba. Rudyard Kipling published his famous *Just So Stories* in 1902, and it is not impossible that the Talmudic story was reframed by someone who had read stories like "How the Camel Got His Hump" (which was translated into Yiddish in 1914), but who? The answer is: I don't know, or, at any rate, can't recall.

If Brooks retold the story to his own child, it would probably have been in the ecumenical version of *Key Largo*, with the unborn child learning the "secrets of the world" rather than those of the Torah. According to his biographer, when his wife, the actress Jean Simmons, asked him if they should bring up their daughter as a Jew, he replied, "Oh, give the kid a break." But that, of course, is merely part of the larger story of the forgetfulness of American Jews.

Take Your Son . . .

GENESIS 22 tells us that "God tested Abraham." That test began with something close to poetry. In the straightforward translation with which Aaron Koller prefaces his thought-provoking new book, *Unbinding Isaac*, God says:

> Now take your son, your only one, whom you love, Isaac, and go to the land of Moriah, and offer him there as a burnt offering on one of the hills, which I will tell you there. (Gen. 22:2)

Why this stately threefold description—"your son, your only one, whom you love"—before Isaac is finally named as the sacrificial victim? Rashi famously paraphrases a midrash that reads the verse as suppressing Abraham's part of a dialogue, as if the readers of Genesis were over-hearing just God's half of a phone conversation:

> He [Abraham] said to Him, "I have two sons." He said to him, "your only son." Abraham said, "this one is an only child of his mother and that one is an only child of his mother." He said to him, "the one you love." He said

to him, "I love both of them." He said to him, "Isaac." And why didn't He reveal it to him from the beginning? In order not to suddenly shock him into confusion and incompetence, and so that he would cherish the commandment and receive a reward for each clause.

In filling in the uncanny gaps and silences of the "Binding of Isaac" (*Akedat Yitzchak*, or simply the Akedah), this midrash and many others tend to demystify it. Abraham, whose only quoted response to God throughout the ordeal is "*hineni*" (literally "here I am," or in the Bible scholar E. A. Speiser's crisp translation, "ready"), becomes a puzzled, obstinate father. In another ancient tradition, which Rashi earlier quotes, God's unfathomable demand is given an exculpatory backstory that cribs from Job: he was tricked into making it by Satan, who questioned Abraham's priorities. Such interpretations betray an anxiety about the Akedah's disturbing power, giving motives and alibis to its protagonists and depriving it of its uncanny force.

Rashi's question about the threefold phrasing of God's request of Abraham is not the first one that occurs to the modern reader of the most terrifying verse in the Hebrew Bible. Nonetheless, the midrashic revelation of a father who insists that he loves both of his sons equally and is perhaps desperately stalling the horrific demand that he can somehow feel coming is, as we now say, relatable. Then again, why should Abraham feel such a demand coming?

In a famous passage, which Koller quotes, Immanuel Kant argued that Abraham should have replied in indignant astonishment "That I ought not kill my good son is quite certain. But that you, this apparition, are God, of that I am not certain." As a child of the Enlightenment, of which Kant is a founding father, I find it easy to agree with him, and yet one also feels that it is a little too easy to do so, that we ought to at least understand what is going on in the biblical narrative before dismissing it. After all, Isaac was not merely Abraham's "good son" or even just the only son (of Sarah), whom he loved, he was the child for whom Abraham had waited a lifetime and through whom God had promised that his line would be continued and become a great nation. Moreover, the idea that God is, in one sense or another, owed not only the first fruits of one's field but the firstborn of every womb, "man and beast," is shot through the Hebrew Bible, as are dramas regarding favorite sons.

To return to Rashi's commentary, why should Abraham be more richly rewarded for forcing God to come to the point? The strangest rabbinic answer to that question of which I am aware is that of Rabbi Isaac of Volozhin, the son and successor of Rabbi Chaim of Volozhin, the leading disciple of the Vilna Gaon and the founder of the first modern yeshiva. In a textually ingenious, if perverse, comment, Reb Itzele, as he was known, argued that Abraham's part of the dialogue should be reread as an argument to sacrifice *both* of his sons. The surprise is that this topsy-turvy version actually works: at each step of the midrashic dialogue, Abraham can now be heard not as dimly groping his way towards understanding God's awful meaning but as understanding it immediately—and then zealously bargaining to sacrifice both Isaac and Ishmael. God says "Take your son," and Abraham's instantaneous response amounts to "why not both?" This is certainly not what either the ancient midrash or the medieval commentator imagined when they staged the scene, but did Reb Itzele nonetheless get something right about the disturbing presuppositions beneath the biblical text? Namely, that Abraham fully acknowledged he had an impossible debt to God that he was prepared to repay.

And what should we make of the fact that just as the hill in Moriah on which Abraham bound Isaac is said to be the future Temple Mount, the Akedah itself is near the center of Judaism? It is recited daily in morning prayers and read publicly on Rosh Hashanah as a reminder to God to deal with his people mercifully because of the merit of "our father Abraham."

AARON KOLLER doesn't mention Reb Itzele's odd commentary (no one does), but a nineteenth-century Christian contemporary of his is at the heart of Koller's argument about the troubling place of the Binding of Isaac in modern Jewish thought. That contemporary is, of course, Søren Kierkegaard.

As Koller takes pains to point out, Kierkegaard's *Fear and Trembling* is an extraordinarily complex book, in which he works and reworks the story of Abraham's trial. The book's title comes from Paul, who told the Corinthians that he did not come to preach to them with reason but rather in "fear and trembling." Kierkegaard's argument similarly dwells insistently on the absurdity of faith. If one doesn't have the courage to say that "faith can make it into a holy deed to murder one's son," Kierkegaard says, then it would be better to be done with the story altogether and let the moral "judgement fall on Abraham as on anyone else," as Kant had argued.

> The ethical expression for what he did is that he was willing to murder Isaac; the religious expression is that he was willing to sacrifice Isaac; but in this contradiction lies the very anguish that can make one sleepless; and yet without that anguish Abraham is not the one he is.

Who was Abraham, according to Kierkegaard? He was a "knight of faith," not because he resigned himself to sacrificing his child—Agamemnon could do that—but because he did so while, in an acrobatic "double-movement" of faith, also believing, absurdly but wholeheartedly, that Isaac would be returned to him.

As Koller points out, this is a thoroughly Christian reading, which presupposes the idea that Isaac's almost-sacrifice and last-second salvation at the hand of "an angel of the Lord," set the historical stage for the death and resurrection of Jesus. In the New Testament's Epistle to the Hebrews, we read: "By faith Abraham, when put to the test, offered up Isaac. . . . He considered the fact that God is able even to raise someone from the dead—and figuratively speaking, he did receive him back" (Heb. 11:17–19). But it is hard to find any hint of this kind of faith in Genesis 22.

Koller makes two other important points about Kierkegaard's interpretation. First, he argues that, for Kierkegaard, the story of the Akedah is essentially about surrendering one's beloved for the higher love one owes to God, rather than about taking that person's life. "The violence in Genesis 22," he writes, "is beside the point in *Fear and Trembling*." This is true at some level. As Clare Carlisle's new biography makes vividly clear, when Kierkegaard wrote of Abraham sacrificing Isaac, he was often thinking of how he had just cut off his engagement to the young Regine Olsen in obedience to some inner spiritual imperative neither she nor his bourgeois contemporaries understood. Nonetheless, I think Koller overstates the point. After all, Kierkegaard repeatedly describes Abraham's almost-act as "murder." Moreover, he prefaces *Fear and Trembling* with several midrash-like variations on the story, including the following:

> When Isaac saw [Abraham's] face a second time it was changed, his gaze was wild, his mien one of horror. He caught Isaac by the chest, threw him to the ground and said: 'Foolish boy, do you believe I am your father? I am an idolater. Do you believe this is God's command? No, it is my

own desire.' Then Isaac trembled and in his anguish cried: 'God in heaven have mercy on me, God of Abraham have mercy on me; if I have no father on earth, then be Thou my father!' But below his breath Abraham said to himself: 'Lord in heaven I thank Thee; it is after all better that he believe that I am a monster than that he lose faith in Thee.'

So, Kierkegaard is attuned to the violence at the center of the Akedah. Still, Koller has a point, which I would amend to say that Kierkegaard had little interest in that violence *as a sacrifice.* Nor was he interested in the specific religious logic of biblical sacrifice.

Koller's second criticism is morally trenchant and central to the argument of his book: Kierkegaard, and the many interpreters who have followed him in concentrating on Abraham's existential dilemma, reduce Isaac to "a mere prop in the story." He brings out the monstrosity of this position in a brief, illuminating discussion of Caravaggio's painting, *The Sacrifice of Isaac* (1603). In the painting (actually Caravaggio's second work with that name to depict the scene), Abraham is holding a terrified teenaged Isaac's neck down on the rough stone altar. The young man stares out at the viewer helplessly, as the ram who will become his substitute ambles placidly into the picture, and an urgent angel grabs Abraham's knife-hand. "Caravaggio," Koller writes, "uses Isaac's eye to break the illusion of tranquility . . . Isaac's screaming gaze forces us to grapple with the fact that as Abraham is becoming 'our father,' Isaac is being murdered."

As Koller notes, the pre-modern Jewish tradition, by contrast, did not forget Isaac. Indeed, when the Akedah came to be taken as a paradigm for Jewish martyrdom, Isaac's willingness to die for God became at least as important as his father's willingness to kill for Him. Thus, Ephraim of Bonn's searing Akedah poem, written in the wake of Jewish martyrdom in the Second and Third Crusades, depicts Isaac as his father's willing partner. In Judah Goldin's translation of Shalom Spiegel's classic study of the poem and its sources, Isaac says, "Bind for me my hands and my feet/Lest I be found wanting and profane the sacrifice." A later stanza describes Isaac dying on the altar before being revived by a "resurrecting dew"—at which point his zealous father tries to kill him again before being stopped by the angel a second time. In the dark midrashic tradition this poem draws upon, Isaac becomes the story's spiritual hero (though this version, too, lets Abraham off the moral hook).

A KEY ELEMENT of Koller's book is his critique of Rabbi Joseph B. Soloveitchik, the central figure in twentieth-century Modern Orthodoxy and the intellectual and spiritual leader of its flagship institution, Yeshiva University, where, as it happens, Koller now teaches. In a number of Soloveitchik's essays, Koller astutely points out, he "describes religion in general as exemplified by retreat, recoil, sacrifice, and self-defeat and describes all of these as exemplified by the Akedah." In short, Soloveitchik seems to have followed Kierkegaard in reading the Akedah as a parable for the existential crisis of the figure he famously called "the lonely man of faith." Certainly, as Koller notes, his descriptions of the Akedah are often openly borrowed from *Fear and Trembling*:

> The enormous feat of the knight of faith was demonstrated not in his actual compliance with the divine order but in the manner in which he behaved in the face of the most puzzling divine absurdity. . . . Abraham did not realize the absurdity and paradoxality of the divine order, which canceled all previous promises and covenants . . . Abraham was great in his acting in accordance with the logic of the absurd.

This passage occurs in the course of a more than 700-word footnote in which Soloveitchik says the Akedah showed that the covenantal relationship was one in which "Man sacrificed himself to God, and God dedicated Himself to man." The man in question is Abraham; Isaac, who was bound to the altar, is never mentioned.

In another essay, in which Soloveitchik takes the Akedah to be the paradigm for prayer, he does talk of Isaac, but in a way that underlines Koller's critique of Kierkegaardian moral blindness. When the angel intervened and a ram was substituted for his son, Abraham's "external drama changed, but the internal drama remained the same."

> Isaac, bound on the altar, turned into a ram, and Isaac was a ram, slaughtered, his blood sprinkled, his body burnt, the ashes were piled on Mount Moriah for generations. The binding of Isaac, which plays such a prominent role in the Jewish liturgy and world-view, means: the binding of man and the sacrifice of him. . . . The spirit of man, clothed in the body of an animal, is sacrificed to God. . . . Build an altar. Arrange the pieces of wood. Kindle the fire. Take the knife and slaughter *your existence* for my sake—thus commands the awesome God. (Italics mine.)

Koller does not deny that such passages may articulate something deep about the kind of passionate prayer that calls for self-negation, but he is at his strongest in showing just how morally troubling and textually implausible they are as readings of Genesis 22. After all, Abraham wasn't sacrificing himself.

Later in the book, Koller quotes Soloveitchik's contemporary Emmanuel Levinas's perceptive criticism of Kierkegaard to great effect. "Perhaps," Levinas wrote of Abraham's response to the intervening angel, his "ear for hearing the voice that brought him back to the ethical order was the highest moment in the drama." Whereas Soloveitchik writes of Abraham's response to the angel as almost irrelevant ("the internal drama remained the same"), Levinas focused on the redemptive third act of the Akedah and the "others" who were there with Abraham at the top of the mountain: the restraining angel and the terrified Isaac.

Koller frames his critique of Soloveitchik and other Kierkegaardians in terms of the dire public consequences of their approach to religion. "Reading Genesis 22 with Kierkegaard," he writes in the concluding chapter, "leads to an inability to explain why someone whose religion obligates them to marry more than one person, or to refuse contraceptive coverage [to others], or to deny vaccinations to their children, or to shoot a mosque full of people, or to fly a plane into a building full of people is wrong."

It's an extraordinary list. One wouldn't have thought that the Catholic Little Sisters of the Poor should be grouped with mass murderers, regardless of what one thinks of their position on employee health care plans. To be fair, Koller immediately notes that he is not drawing an equivalency among the religious bad actors he lists. But he does insist that the stakes are high, because "many people do seek guidance in biblical stories." However, he cites not a single instance when anything remotely like such religious terrorism or even incivility has actually been justified by an existentialist reading of the Akedah.

Koller's framing leads one to expect to read of some deeply problematic Jewish legal ruling or theologically driven moral lapse on the part of Soloveitchik or some other prominent Jewish Kierkegaardian. The closest he comes is to quote an academic article that mentions an Israeli rabbi who wrote, "Are we not obligated to the Torah's laws even when they appear, in human eyes, to be unethical norms?" I have no doubt that I prefer Koller's religious humanism to the apparent position of this unnamed (and almost certainly un-Kierkegaardian) rabbi. Still, the reader was led to expect more. Moreover, while Jewish law, like all legal systems, may come into tension with the dictates of morality, it cannot be equated with the existential brain-fire of some "lonely man of faith." Perhaps the problem in reading Genesis 22 with Kierkegaard is just that it is ultimately a bad reading, textually and morally obtuse, as Koller has shown, but without implications for public policy.

UNBINDING ISAAC is a lucid thesis-driven tour of some of the most important interpretations of the Akedah. Although I don't know if it was, I imagine it as one of those books that began as a terrific undergraduate class in which a central question is traced through a dazzling, dizzying series of texts and thinkers, ending with a sketch of the teacher's own speculative answer.

Koller's own reading of the Akedah takes off from the interpretation of the fourteenth-century commentator Joseph ibn Kaspi. Ibn Kaspi took Maimonides's somewhat counterintuitive statement in the *Guide of the Perplexed* that Abraham's hearing of God's original demand was a lower form of prophecy than his response to the angel who stayed his hand. The first was like an equivocal dream vision, while the second was a more direct prophecy. Ibn Kaspi supported this interpretation by noting that, in fact, two different names of God are used in the story. When God makes his terrible request, He is identified as Elohim, the generic biblical term for God, but the intervening angel is described as "the messenger of the Lord," that is, the divine being as designated by His proper, or "explicit," name, the Tetragrammaton. This makes sense, Ibn Kaspi says, because Isaac's sacrifice was "in fact, not desired by the Lord." And when the "angel of the Lord" says to Abraham, "Don't stretch your hand against the boy, and do not do anything to him, for now I know that you are a fearer of

God, as you have not spared your son, your only one, from me," he was speaking quite precisely because it wasn't really *the Lord* who made the original demand, it was just God, or rather Abraham's dim, imperfect perception of Him.

Koller takes this claim in a more passional or personalist way than Ibn Kaspi would have been likely to when he summarizes that "God wants child sacrifice, as an expression of love and commitment. But God *more* does not want it, as a reflection of a higher value." That higher value, he goes on to argue, is the biblical recognition that children are not the property of their parents: "children, like all other human beings, cannot be mere adjuncts in someone else's religious experience." This is, I think, a profound teaching; we have all seen children—or, to put it less dramatically, their childhoods—sacrificed on the altar of parental desires, including spiritual ones. But is this the teaching of the Akedah?

I am not so sure. Or, rather, since Genesis 22 overpowers and confounds all interpretations in the end, let me briefly note some of my qualms about Koller's reading by returning to the question of how Abraham understood God's terrible request and why it would have made sense to him (or to the earliest readers of the Akedah). Koller describes the ancient desire to sacrifice one's child as a misguided "expression of love and commitment," and he describes the practice of ancient Near Eastern child sacrifice and the Bible's somewhat ambivalent attitude toward it. But he spends little time on the biblical preoccupation with first-born and favorite sons and the way in which they specifically are owed to God. Israel itself is, after all, described as God's "firstborn son," and it becomes so only after Abraham has passed the test, because, the angel tells him, "you have not spared your son, your only one." What seems missing to me in reassuring interpretations of the Akedah such as Koller's is that they read it as eradicating the notion of a father's debt to God as a religious mistake. In contrast, the Bible itself returns to the idea obsessively, almost inevitably subverting or sublimating it, but never simply giving it up.

The fifth chapter of *Pirkei Avot* (Ethics of the Fathers) teaches that ten things were created on the evening of the first Sabbath. Among them, some authorities include "the ram of our father Abraham," which is to say that from the outset of creation an animal substitute was intended for Isaac but not that the trial itself was a mistake. Elsewhere, we learn that the horn of that same ram was the one blown at Sinai. The blasts of the shofar at Rosh Hashanah, it would seem, recall not only the revelation at Sinai but our father Abraham's attempt to repay his terrifying, yet obscurely comprehensible debt to God.

Salsa and Sociology

As a CHILD of eight or nine, I evolved a theory about different kinds of Jews, based, more or less, on the hot sauce we kept on our table. The brand of salsa my mother always bought featured a picture of a thermometer on the side. The mercury in this thermometer rose from Mild to Medium to Hot, and it occurred to me, for I thought as a child, that the three basic kinds of Jews—or more precisely synagogues to which the Jews I knew belonged—could be placed on a similar continuum. Reform Jews were Mild, Conservative Jews were Medium, and Orthodox Jews were Hot.

If pressed to say what I thought was being measured that was supposed to be analogous to the heat of chili peppers, I guess that I would have said something about the amount of "Jewish stuff" one did or was required to do. If pressed further, I probably would have put my family somewhere between Medium and Hot. The theory was descriptive, not prescriptive. As far as I can remember, I had no desire to be the religious equivalent of tongue-scaldingly habanero-hot.

Around this time, my mother drove us across the Bay Bridge to participate in a rally for Soviet Jews at Emanu-El, the big, old Reform Temple in San Francisco, which was founded in 1850. By American Jewish standards it's practically a medieval cathedral. Certainly that's what it felt like to me. You could fit half a dozen of our little East Bay *shuls* inside it, and the pillars stretching up to a magnificently vaulted ceiling seemed as tall to me as the redwoods of Berkeley's Tilden Park, if not the cedars of Lebanon. This, together with other experiences, spurred me to add a corollary to my theory: The wealth of synagogues was inversely proportional to their religious "heat."

My childish religious heat map fit the folk taxonomy implicit in the everyday speech of American Jews pretty well. Thus, when I heard someone describing himself or others as "very Reform," it never meant that prophetic ideals of justice were discussed at the dinner table, or that the works of the great liberal historian-theologian Abraham Geiger were on the bookshelf. It meant that they did not lead markedly Jewish lives. There is even a whole class of predictable Jewish jokes based on this: "How Reform are they? So Reform that . . . ," and then a punchline about, say, eating ham and cheese on Yom Kippur.

At some point, however, I put away my childish theories. I met learned and serious liberal Jews on the one hand and prayed in imposing, wealthy Orthodox synagogues on the other. Moreover, when I later studied the ideological origins of the different modern Jewish movements, I came to understand that there was no single scale on which they all could be ranged. The architects of the Reform movement did not regard themselves as "Very Mild" on some halakhic heat scale; the Conservative movement did not concede that they were any less devout in their commitment to Jewish law, properly—that is, historically—understood, than the Orthodox, not to speak of Reconstructionism and the many varieties of Jewish secularism, including classical Zionism.

And yet. In some respects, my salsa sociology explained parts of my particular American Jewish experience better than the ideological self-understandings of the movements. For instance, I've known many *ba'alei teshuvah*, who have "returned" to traditional religious practice, sometimes moving from Reform through Conservative Judaism before arriving at Orthodoxy. Rarely, even among intellectuals, is such a move best characterized as one in which the *ba'al teshuvah* first thinks that halakha (Jewish law) is no longer the best way to express Jewish social and spiritual ideals in the modern world, then decides that it is but that halakha must be understood as a dynamic historical process, and, finally, comes to believe in an eternal law revealed at Sinai.

A better description of the process is that such people increasingly wanted their everyday lives to be determined by their Judaism, and they found this in Orthodox communities of one kind or another. I think this is also true of the many people I've known who grew up in the Conservative movement (Solomon Schechter schools, Camp Ramah, etc.) and now find themselves identifying as Orthodox. The great sociologist Émile Durkheim spoke of "social facts," beliefs, norms, and practices with the power to structure individual lives. One way to describe what the *ba'al teshuvah* is looking for is a way to make his or her Judaism into a real, brute social fact.

I was talking about this with a prominent American-Israeli journalist the other day, who said "Sure, if you want to be totally Jewish, you've got three choices: You can become a Reform or Conservative *rabbi*, you can become Orthodox—or you can make *aliyah*." One could object that one can also become a professor of Jewish studies, but that's not really a counter-example, since there are only a few hundred of us. The best counter-example comes from the world of independent *minyanim*, in which many participants live intensely Jewish lives of ritual, study, and prayer while retaining a non-Orthodox approach to belief and practice. Whether the *minyanim*, and allied institutions such as *Mechon Hadar* and *Limmud*, can alter the social dynamics of American Jewry remains to be seen.

TWO REALIZATIONS dawned on me in reading the Pew Research Center's recent report, "A Portrait of Jewish Americans." The first was just how small a Jewish bubble I have been living in. While I've been praying in Orthodox *shuls* with *ba'alei teshuvah* and Ramah campers, the American Jewish world has been swiftly moving in the opposite direction. As the report states:

> Within all three denominational movements, most of the switching is in the direction of less-traditional Judaism . . . one-quarter of people who were raised Orthodox have since become Conservative or Reform Jews, and 28% of those raised Reform have left the ranks of Jews by religion entirely.

One feels the sheer gravitational force of American Jewish life in such sentences. By contrast, the move in the other direction begins to look insignificant, a counter-cultural trickle.

My other realization was, of course, that my childish theory was closer to the truth than my later, sophisticated adult view of American Jewish life. The religious ideologies that I had taken so seriously as an adult now look epiphenomenal, like froth on the waves. Take, for instance, the following question posed by the Pew researchers: "How important is religion in your life?" Eighty-three percent of Orthodox Jews answered very important, less than half of Conservative Jews (forty-three percent) agreed, and only sixteen percent of Reform Jews responded that religion was very important to them. Of Jews with no denominational affiliation the number was eight percent.

Since the Pew researchers were certainly not defining the religion in question as Orthodoxy, it is hard not to conclude that some like it Hot and we call those Jews Orthodox, and some like it Mild, and we call those Jews Reform. Conservative Jews find themselves in the rapidly shrinking middle. As for the Jews of "no religion," these would appear to be not Jewish secularists (as the Pew researchers sometimes sort of imply) but mostly Jews looking for the exit.

Hello, I Must Be Going

JAMES LOEFFLER'S ESSAY, "The Death of Jewish Culture," by which he means secular Jewish culture, is a compelling *tour de force*, which is to say that it says something important and says it with style but also that, in the swoop and slash of its argument, it leaves out a fair bit.

The occasion for Loeffler's reflections is the demise over the last few years of several high-profile projects aimed at promoting Jewish culture to young (or at least young-ish) artsy American Jewish hipsters. However, as Loeffler's choice of presiding spirits—he quotes the cultural Zionist Ahad Ha'am, his friend the great Hebrew poet Hayyim Nahman Bialik, and the Yiddish folklorist-playwright S. An-sky—shows, the Jewish culture he is really eulogizing is not only high and secular but distinctly Eastern European—and it has been gone for three-quarters of a century. The kind of secular culture he is interested in is a "self-consciously modern, public culture, rooted in the unique civilization that gave it birth and formed its voice, and expressive of a thick, expansive, holistic identity."

No one, not its programmers, not its funders, and certainly not Professor Loeffler, ever thought that Makor, the now-defunct New York Jewish "nightclub-cum-gallery" with which he begins, would anchor *that* kind of culture. Art and literature that express a "thick, expansive, holistic identity" take, if not a *shtetl*, at the very least a shared way of life: rituals, symbols, a vocabulary; a recognizable ethos and a common set of problems. In short, they require a distinctive, bounded culture, in the anthropological sense of the word.

The whole philanthropic point of projects like Makor is to address the fact that young Jewish Americans are, first of all, Americans. In the absence of a strong religious identity, they are liable not only to like precisely the same novels, songs, and movies as their non-Jewish peers at Harvard, the University of Virginia, or Oberlin but also to date and marry those peers when they graduate and move to Brooklyn or the Upper West Side. If, the thinking goes, they could become more interested in Jewish things, broadly and secularly construed, the latter eventuality—that is, assimilation and intermarriage—would be a little less likely. And if, in the process, one could foster the career of a brilliant musician or fund a quirky but watchable indie film, well, then, all the better. This may or may not be a good use of philanthropic dollars—it all depends on how much one likes "gleaming . . . postmodern sanctuaries" of culture like the late Makor and how highly one values the project of encouraging those with relatively thin Jewish identities to make them slightly thicker.

Loeffler knows all of this. His real purpose, I think, is to remind us of what a truly secular Jewish culture once looked like, and the conditions under which it flourished. With regard to the latter, there seems to me to be a paradox, but more on that later.

WHEN AN-SKY CALLED for a secular Jewish culture, saying that the "people of the shofar must become the people of the clarinet," one wonders whether he realized quite how completely the shofar, and the meanings carried by its blasts, could disappear from Jewish consciousness, or quite how impossible it would be for a people to be defined by their devotion to clarinets (or culture). This is not to underestimate An-sky, who was no sentimentalist, but Loeffler's use of his aphorism does call to mind two historical anecdotes that might be said to bracket the creation and demise of secular Ashkenazi culture.

Sometime in the 1780s, Rabbi Raphael Kohen, the chief rabbi of the Jewish "triple community" of Altona, Hamburg, and Wandsbeck, summoned Solomon Maimon to come see him. Maimon was a twenty-something Talmudic genius, lapsed rabbi, and would-be philosopher who had taken up residence at a nearby liberal secondary school (*Gymnasium*) to study mathematics, science, classical languages, and European literature. In short, he was trying to get cultured—and to get away from a culture. Maimon tells the story of their confrontation in his classic *Autobiography*:

> We entered into a wide-ranging debate. . . . Because this method wasn't getting him anywhere with me, he turned to sermonizing. When it, too, failed to produce results, he worked himself up into a holy fervor, and he began to shout: Shofar! Shofar! . . . While shouting, he pointed to a shofar that happened to be lying on the table, and he asked me: "Do you know what that is?" I riposted audaciously: "Oh, sure; it's a ram's horn." These words made the rabbi tumble back into his chair. He began to utter lamentations for my lost soul. Leaving him to lament for as long as he wanted to, I said good-bye.

It is audacious to reduce a shofar to "a ram's horn" only when both the speaker and his audience know that sounds of the shofar were heard at Sinai, that the shofar was blown in the Temple, that it calls one to repentance on Rosh Hashanah, and that it is blown on the occasion of an excommunication (which may have been what Rabbi Kohen had in mind). And one can only exit in insouciant triumph—and then tell the story—if the rabbi and the religion he represents retain at least some of their power.

Many of the great works of secular Jewish culture (of which Maimon's *Autobiography* is an early instance) derive their energy from this heretical dynamic. They are not only "rooted in the unique civilization" that gave birth to them, they are also actively rebelling against it. Their voices were formed by this civilization, but their art—especially their distinctively Jewish art—often consists in raising those voices in protest against (or irony about) the tradition. Secular poets like Bialik (or, later, Yehuda Amichai) were always just leaving.

Then there are those who have already left. In 1938, the great jazz clarinetist Artie Shaw (formerly Arshawksy) and his band appeared on a radio show to play their hit tune "Nightmare," which had a klezmerish feel. The virtuoso classical violinist Efrem Zimbalist, who had begun his career as a Russian Jewish prodigy at the turn of the century, was waiting in the wings as the next guest. Despite his disdain for jazz, Zimbalist picked up his violin and joined in unannounced, like an extra fiddler at a village wedding.

Even if, as the critic Nat Hentoff once claimed, Shaw had a *nigun* in mind when he composed "Nightmare" (which makes one wonder at the title), and even if the sound of the notes plucked Zimbalist's Ashkenazi heartstrings, this seems as good a moment as any to mark when the people of the shofar became the people of the clarinet and, just to that extent, stopped being a people in all but the most vestigial sense. Zimbalist and Shaw may have "bageled" each other as the band swung, but it didn't mean a thing, or at least not very much. Give these guys an artistic residency at Makor, some gushy profiles in the popular Jewish media, and it could almost have been the twenty-first century.

Solomon Maimon and Artie Shaw were both cool cats, but what makes Maimon a figure in the history of Jewish culture and Shaw a footnote in Jewish trivia—"who was Ava Gardner's Jewish husband?"—is that Maimon couldn't escape.

Of course, what killed An-sky's European secular Jewish culture was not American-style acculturation, it was Nazi genocide, and it is impossible to say what would have happened to it (or to us) had history taken a different, gentler course. But therein lies the paradox to which I alluded earlier. There is a real question—perhaps it is just the Jewish version of the classic modernist question—of how long a culture can sustain itself on the rebellion against its predecessor.

Can American Jews create a distinctively secular Jewish culture? Loeffler holds out hope, albeit faint, that "one or two geniuses" might yet spark a renaissance. Given his description of such a culture as necessarily "rooted in the unique civilization that gave it birth," I am struck by another, somewhat paradoxical thought. Such geniuses may be most likely to emerge from the sort of present-day Orthodox worlds in which Ahad Ha'am, Bialik, and An-sky are decidedly *not* names with which to conjure—worlds, however, that these figures themselves would have easily recognized. If secular Jewish culture ever makes a comeback, it will be in rebellion.

Hebrew School Days

WHEN I WAS nineteen, I saw an ad at the UCLA Career Center for a job teaching "Jewish history through drama," at the Sunday school of a large nearby temple. It was only a couple of hours a week, but it paid maybe four times as much as my job at the Student Store. I had never taught Jewish history or anything else, but I had acted in a student production of Beckett's *Endgame* that summer. (I was Hamm, or maybe it was Clov.)

At the interview, it turned out that the school director, who I'll call Lisa, had, as far as I could tell, no idea what she meant by "Jewish history through drama." There was no particular period she wanted covered, no book she had in mind, and no theory of how to teach acting, or Jewish history for that matter, to junior high schoolers. But she was duly impressed with the Beckett, and she found the fact that I had been in a yeshiva only two years earlier fascinating.

Mainly, she wanted to talk about her study of "Hasidic philosophy" with a local Chabad rabbi. I nodded politely and didn't try to disabuse her of the idea that studying the *Tanya* in Bel-Air was very much like studying Talmud in

Jerusalem, even if black hats played a role in both experiences. I also learned that the temple's school had won awards for innovation and excellence, and that I would be required to accompany my students on a weekend Shabbaton in the spring.

Those first Sunday mornings were terrifying. My half-baked idea had been to introduce them to some obscure and exciting episode of Jewish history and then find a way to dramatize it. Having read a little (very little) of Gershom Scholem, I thought that the story of the false messiah Shabbtai Zevi would be a good idea—it wasn't. Given that the kids were iffy on King David (and Jesus for that matter) and had never really thought about the idea of a messiah, personal or otherwise, the seventeenth-century adventures of a melancholic mystic in the Mediterranean was a tough sell. I remember once looking wildly out of my classroom window as Lisa approached while fourteen-year-old boys and girls slammed into each other in an exuberant Punk Rock interpretation of a Turkish Sabbatean mob. She returned my look blandly and marched right past the classroom door.

Of course, I had gone to Hebrew school—that's what we always called it though very little Hebrew was ever learned—through most of elementary school. I'd walk the five blocks down Bancroft from Berkeley's Washington Elementary School to Congregation Beth Israel (fading orange-red bricks, worn-wood floor, and Israeli and American flags flanking the *aron kodesh*), where a part of the sanctuary was partitioned off to make a classroom from four to six on Tuesday and Thursday afternoons.

Even at nineteen, not much of that experience had stuck with me, certainly not enough to be of help with lesson plans. I remembered a glamorous Israeli teacher named Varda teaching us that the word for chalk was *gir*, with an exciting back-of-the-throat trill for the "r" sound, and that the word for chalkboard was the same as the one used to describe the tablets on which the Ten Commandments were inscribed. And I remembered Rabbi Leibowitz coming into class to show us the way the strings and knots of the *tzitzis* on a *tallis* could be added up to 613, the number of commandments in the Torah. And I remembered impudently climbing out the window with a friend when another teacher turned to the chalkboard. But mostly I remembered playing touch football before and between classes out in the middle of the street with Jake and Steve, one-on-one (it was a small class) with Jake as all-time quarterback. We'd diagram the plays on our palms, and then Jake would run around Kenny Stabler-like, joyfully, but pointlessly (no one was rushing him), while Steve or I tried to get open for the down-and-out bullet or the long bomb. More than anything else, for me Hebrew school was running down Jefferson Avenue with Jake's rainbow pass soaring above me and little Stevie Klein showing me his heels as the afternoon light faded and the sweet, earnest Rabbi Lifsics called us to come back inside.

Actually, touch football turned out be more useful for my teaching than my distinguished career on the stage. I settled into a pattern of turning some passage from the weekly Torah portion into a kind of playlet and playing sports with the kids during the break between classes. As the year wore on, Lisa occasionally spoke with me about her idea of bringing all the kids to Chabad for the Spring Shabbaton to observe "a different form of spirituality." But when the announcement of our destination came, it turned out that, somewhere along the line, plans had changed radically.

We were going to St. Andrew's, a Benedictine retreat in the San Gabriel Mountains outside of Los Angeles, to celebrate the Sabbath with the monks. After the announcement, Lisa took me aside to warn me that the change in plans meant that I would need to bring my own food if I wanted to keep kosher. On Friday night we met some of the monks, lit candles, and had a Shabbat dinner. It turned out that one of my students, Maurice P.—a speedy wide receiver—also kept kosher, or at least thought he did, or perhaps he just thought he should keep me company. We split my take-out order of fried chicken and challa from the Kosher Kolonel.

The next morning, the rabbi came to spend the day with the kids. We met him in the parking lot as he drove up. He took a Torah out of his hatchback and led us all to a little clearing in the woods, where he laid it gently on the ground as he told us that two hundred years ago the holy Ba'al Shem Tov had prayed in the woods. Then he unscrolled the Torah to that week's portion and, using a twig as a pointer, read a few verses. When he finished, he said (perhaps thinking of the Lubavitchers we weren't visiting or even the Benedictines we were), "You know, kids, some people think that every word of the Torah is priceless, like a diamond, but we don't think that. We believe," he said, gesturing at the California scrub around him, "that the Torah is like a diamond *mine*, and you've got to clear away all the rubble to get at the diamonds." It's actually not a bad description of classic nineteenth-century liberal religion in the light of biblical criticism with a twist of Buber, but I've often wondered what, if anything, he was trying to teach those particular LA kids with their tiny fund of Jewish knowledge.

At lunch, sloppy joes were served. The rabbi and one of the monks led a somewhat desultory theological conversation about images of God to which the students paid less than full attention. Afterward we had a rousing game of touch football. The following morning, we observed, but did not partake in, Communion, and took the bus back to West Los Angeles. Not long after Shabbat at the monastery, Lisa told me that it was time to provide written assessments of each of my students for the year. This baffled me. I was certain that she couldn't possibly want academic grades. (Had I received grades in Hebrew school? I couldn't remember.) Eventually I decided that what she must be requesting were assessments of the students themselves. I picked up a grade card, looked at the name, and wrote, "Maurice P. is a very fine football player."

Books vs. Children

IN THE SECOND VOLUME of his big biography of Saul Bellow, Zachary Leader quotes Bellow's agent Harriet Wasserman's description of an excruciating moment at a Nobel Prize after-party. At the end of the meal, Bellow's Swedish publisher rose to toast him, then Daniel, Bellow's twelve-year-old son, got up: "I'd just like to say my father has been so busy, but he still had time for me. Thanks, Pop."

Then his oldest son, Gregory, rose to speak:

> "My young brother has given me the courage to say something I've always wanted to say." . . . Greg was standing there, his walrus mustache trembling slightly. "I never thought you loved me, and I never understood what the creative process was. You were behind a closed door all the time, writing, listening to Mozart." He was looking straight at his father. "I was young. I didn't know what you were doing behind the closed door." . . . All the European publishers, all of them men, were sitting very stiff and upright. . . . Looks of total shock—horror almost—on their faces. . . . "And then . . ." Greg was barely controlling himself. ". . . I witnessed the birth of my own child and I

understood what the creative process was, and I understood then that you really did love me."

A stunned silence followed; Bellow walked over to his middle child, Adam, shook his hand and said, "Thanks, kid, for not saying anything," and left.

Recently, Rivka Galchen, a novelist and new mother, has cast a skeptical eye on stories about the trauma of the writer-parent's closed door.

> There is a certain consistency of complaint . . . the child comes to show something to the writer-parent . . . during the daytime hours, and the writer-parent says to the child, I can't right now, I'm working. There are also often descriptions of the looming, hostile, uncompromising door of the home office. Apparently it is very troubling for children to see their parents working, at least doing the kind of work that does not make itself visibly obvious.

Galchen's skepticism is twofold: She doubts that this happens as often as it is described in the memoirs of the children of authors, and she wonders what the big deal is. After all, most parents work, and why should making up stories in the other room be any more mysterious or troubling to a child than office work?

These are reasonable questions, but Galchen, who wrote these words after having her first baby, knows that there is something deeper in the rivalry between books and children, something that Gregory Bellow was getting at in the agitated, inchoate talk of creativity, birth, and babies with which he toasted (roasted?) his father. In fact, it is pretty much what Galchen's book *Little Labors* is about.

Montaigne says a terrible thing that puts the issue starkly. In his essay "Of the Affection of Fathers for their Children," he wonders whether an author wouldn't prefer to "bury his children . . . than the fruits of his mind." To be fair to Montaigne, this was probably a macabre and unconscious consolation for the fact that all but one of his children died in infancy. On the other hand, he did have a theory: Since we love our children as second selves, loving them precisely because we have produced them, we—or at least the writers and artists among us—should remember that we also produce something else from ourselves, which are "products of a part more noble than the body and . . . more purely our own."

> In this act of generation we are both mother and father; these "children" cost us dearer and, if they are any good, bring us more honour. In the case of our other children their good qualities belong much more to them than to us: we have only a very slight share in them; but in the case of these, all their grace, worth and beauty belong to us. For this reason they have a more lively resemblance and correspondence to us. Plato adds that such children are immortal and immortalize their fathers.

Montaigne's mistake—and, to some extent, that of the pained young Gregory Bellow trying to understand his brilliant, bemedaled father—is to equate artistic creation with biological procreation, clever artifacts with human beings. Sitting behind a closed door writing words is not really at all like giving birth. To think that it is risks a kind of idolatry. In doing so, one ascribes infinite value to a merely human thing, a verbal contraption, and risks sacrificing a child—who really does have infinite value—to that thing.

In this case Moloch is the father's book. But maybe this is all a little overwrought. As Rivka Galchen implicitly points out, one can also harm or ignore one's children in the pursuit of less romantic professions. Do doctors and lawyers see *more* of their children than authors? And how bad is a closed door anyway?

Still, there is something troubling about the way writers often talk about their work and their children, and it probably won't do to just point out that other occupations can also skew one's priorities. Too often, writers, especially male writers, think of their books as in competition with their children, or imagine, with Montaigne, that they are their children. (When Theodor Adorno sent Gershom Scholem a copy of his *Negative Dialectics*, he fondly called it his "fat child"—something neither scholar was fortunate enough to have, or perhaps wise enough to want.)

IN MY SOPHOMORE and junior years of college, I had a slightly older friend named Adrian, who, like me, aspired to be a writer. When my girlfriend and I told him, and some other friends, that we were going to have a baby and get married, he looked like I had punched him in the stomach. "I need some air," he said and staggered out of the co-op. A couple of days later, I found a xerox of an essay called "Fires," by the then-reigning short-story writer Raymond Carver in my mailbox, inscribed in Adrian's elegant hand. "Mazel Tov to you and Shoshana," he wrote. "Although it might not seem so at first, I find this essay somehow hopeful."

It wasn't. Midway through the essay, Carver says that "I really don't feel that anything happened in my life until I was twenty and married and had kids," but he's not talking about anything good. "I have to say that the greatest single influence on my life and on my writing, directly and indirectly, has been my two children," he writes, before going on to say that "there wasn't any area of my life where their heavy and often baleful influence didn't reach." In the penultimate paragraph he writes about his despair even after getting published in *Esquire*: "my kids were in full cry then . . . and they were eating me alive."

I guess that it's surprising that I invited Adrian to our wedding; surprising too that in all his faux stoic fury and self-pity Carver never mentioned that throughout the years in which his children were "eating him alive," he was, in fact, a violent alcoholic.

And yet, it is true that it is hard to concentrate on big projects while taking care of small children. In a comment on a verse in Proverbs, the Vilna Gaon writes that a true hero is someone who studies Torah day and night, and when his family cries out "'bring us something to support and sustain us,' . . . he pays no attention at all to them nor heeds their voice . . . for he has denied all love except to that of the Lord and His Torah." Presumably, a closed study door would come in handy here.

The Gaon's remark is idiosyncratic and extreme, but one sees this set of priorities in less extreme form elsewhere in the rabbinic tradition and among religious saints, at least of a certain kind, more generally. All-consuming intellectual passions tend to come at the price of children, and artists, scholars, even saints, have too often reveled in their heroic choice to press on with the task. Yeats famously says that

> The intellect of man is forced to choose
> Perfection of the life, or of the work
> And if it take the second must refuse
> A heavenly mansion, raging in the dark.

But neither lives nor works can be perfect, and the thought that they could be is part of the problem.

There is a nice story about the Vilna Gaon's great Hasidic contemporary Rabbi Schneur Zalman of Liadi, his son, Rabbi Dov Ber, and his grandchild. Rabbi Dov Ber and his family were living with his father on the first floor of a two-story house. One evening while Dov Ber was studying, one of his children fell out of the crib. Oblivious, he continued to study as his child cried. Rabbi Schneur Zalman was also studying, but he came down from the second floor, calmed his grandchild, and then went to speak with his son. He told him that one should never be so absorbed in thought that one cannot hear a child's cry. In other words, next time leave the door open.

Exit, Loyalty . . . Crowdsource?

I awoke to the smell of ammonia. I was on my feet, but couldn't remember where. . . . I exhaled instinctively . . . and held my breath for as long as I could. When the air rushed back in, the wet burlap hood fastened around my neck pressed against my cracked lips. I tasted urine, and the reality began flooding back. I was hunched low, in an underground cell, my shaved head scraping through the burlap against a jagged stone ceiling. . . .

Orientation: I remembered that my dungeon cell was four stories underground. I had counted my steps over the days. I could faintly hear the echoes of angry curses issued in Arabic, iron doors slamming, beatings, and cries. They were likely coming from minus two, where I believed my teammates were being held.

Not a single member of the community that had raised me to adulthood knew where I was. I was more alone than I had ever been, but driven by a conviction that eclipsed my solitude. . . . This was the right place for me. . . . I took a moment to recognize the absurdity of my gratitude at the threshold of the interrogation chamber, and caught myself smiling softly under the hood. That conviction was born . . . at Phillips Exeter Academy in 1986.

IT IS A BIT of a surprise to open a big-think policy book on the fate of the Jewish people and read a Jason Bourne scene with a prep-school payoff, but author Tal Keinan is entitled to it. It was a training exercise in the Israeli Air Force, which he joined after moving to Israel, a process that began when, as a junior at Phillips Exeter named Tal Weiner, he started to think seriously about what it meant to be Jewish. Keinan tacks between autobiography and policy throughout *God Is in the Crowd*. Despite his extraordinary achievements—he became an F-16 fighter pilot before getting a Harvard MBA and cofounding the investment firm Clarity Capital—he does so with modesty (the only combat mission he describes is one in which he bombed the wrong target).

The Jewish issues Keinan addresses could not be larger: the accelerating demographic decline of American Jewry, the dangerous sociopolitical stalemate in which Israeli Jews find themselves, and the relation between the two. He describes himself as "an insider in two worlds who had achieved escape velocity from both," and, though he is not unique in this respect, it does give him, as he says, "an uncommon vantage point." Keinan goes on to say that history has proved "that there was one identity I could not escape. I was a Jew," but he knows that even if this proved to be true for him, it is very far from true of American Jewry. As the economist Albert O. Hirschman elegantly showed, there is always the possibility of leaving any organization that demands loyalty. For twenty-first-century American Jews, the exit door is always accessible. As an alternative to exiting an organization, Hirschman pointed out another option, "voice": A citizen or customer can point out flaws, protest, suggest a solution. It is to Keinan's great credit that he sees the Jewish people as a whole and voices his concerns on both the Israeli and the American fronts.

Keinan describes his father's mute fury when his older brother announced his engagement to his non-Jewish girlfriend. Eventually, he took Tal and his three brothers out for dinner to finally, incoherently, tell them how important being Jewish was to him.

> It was Passover, and we were eating pizza as we debated the value of Jewish tradition. The unintended irony was completely consistent with our upbringing. . . . Where was the line between observing a kosher Passover and marrying out of the tribe? We were Jewish, but were we not American as well?

Keinan is clear that he does not fault those Jews who find love outside the faith, as, eventually, each of his three brothers did. However, he correctly insists that the implications for American Jewry as a whole are stark. According to the 2013 Pew Center study of American Jewry, fifty-eight percent of American Jews who get married marry non-Jews (subtract Orthodox Jews from the equation and the number skyrockets to over seventy percent). Among the forty-two percent of American Jews who do marry other Jews (and this includes converts to Judaism), the average number of children is 1.9, which is the same rate for Americans as a whole.

If this trend continues, "the size of the next generation of American Jews who have two Jewish parents will be only 36 percent the size of today's." The following generation, Keinan writes, "will be 13 percent the size of today's— almost complete collapse." This may unfairly discount the Jewish lives and identities of the children of intermarriage, but there are numbers on that too, and they aren't encouraging. The grand story of American Jewry, which now accounts for almost half of world Jewry, could be effectively over within the space of a lifetime, save for a few small enclaves of committed Jews, the majority of them Orthodox, and most of those haredi. One is reminded of the economist Herbert Stein's famous law: "If something cannot go on forever, then it will stop."

WHAT OF ISRAEL, where the other half of world Jewry lives? Simplifying for an American popular audience, Keinan divides Israeli Jewry into three ideological camps: Secularists, Territorialists, and Theocrats. In the Secularist group, he includes not only the heirs of Herzl and Ben-Gurion but all those Israeli Jews, including Modern Orthodox ones, who believe in a fairly strict separation between religion and state. Territorialists are those Religious Zionists who insist that Judea and Samaria should be wholly annexed on theological grounds regardless of the consequences. The Theocrats represent the rapidly growing haredi population, whose primary allegiance is to their own community and their conception of Torah.

Keinan is a frank secularist, but his definition of secularism is overbroad, since it includes all Israelis who accept a (mostly) secular state, religious pluralism, and the possibility of territorial compromise. While he describes the selfless idealism of some of his Religious Zionist fellow soldiers with real admiration, he argues that annexing the territories would quickly lead to a non-Jewish majority in Israel. He shows no understanding of, or sympathy for, the Theocrats, who are, on Keinan's account, haredi free-riders who take a disproportionate amount of government services while refusing to serve in the army and failing to adequately contribute to the economy. Moreover, in addition to what economists call rent-seeking, their political activity is primarily aimed at coercing their fellow citizens to conform to their strict construals of Jewish law concerning matters of personal status, such as marriage, divorce, and conversion. (Keinan and his wife avoided an official rabbinate marriage by having a civil marriage in New York before their non-state-recognized Reform marriage in Israel.)

Even though the Secularists bear "the bulk of both the defense burden and the economic burdens that underpin Israel's survival," they are losing, demographically and politically, and this very loss further undermines their commitment to the Zionist project. He points out that half of all first-graders in Israel are now either haredim or Arab Israelis, meaning that absent a huge cultural shift, they won't be receiving a draft notice in ten years. "In light of the looming defeat of their vision," Keinan writes, "it is becoming difficult for Israel's Secularists to justify shouldering this growing burden." After all, why not just leave for America? (This won't strengthen American Jewry, by the way. As Keinan notes, expatriate Israelis are even more likely to intermarry than American Jews.)

Keinan's analysis alternates between the anecdotal and the schematic, and his broad characterizations obscure a great deal. It is true, for instance, that the secular ideology of the Zionist founders is no longer ascendant, but that doesn't mean that a majority of the country now rejects the idea of a modern pragmatic state. There are also relevant developments that he does not discuss, including the rise of the new "Jewsraeli" identity described by Shmuel Rosner and Camil Fuchs, which combines a soft traditionalism with unwavering patriotism, and there are some encouraging signs of haredi integration into general society. He also ignores recent strategic developments in the Middle East, especially the Sunni states' new posture toward Israel and the chaotic state of Palestinian politics, which influence when and how to negotiate over the territories regardless of whether the Territorialists are right in their eschatological interpretation of history. But he's also not wrong about the danger of the cultural and political divides by which Israel is riven. The Jewish state is lurching toward what, as I write in early December 2019, looks like one of three bad options: an unstable "unity government" of fierce opponents, a narrow government that isn't much more stable, or a third election in eleven months.

If American Jewry is on the verge of evaporating while Israel is about to implode, what is Tal Keinan's solution?

IN 1906 THE BRITISH STATISTICIAN Francis Galton went to a county fair where some 800 people were placing bets on the weight of a fat ox. Some of the contestants were farmers and butchers, but nonexperts who just liked a good bet also competed. No one correctly guessed the weight of the ox, but when Galton averaged all the guesses, he found that their collective wisdom was that the ox was 1,197 pounds. It weighed 1,198. As James Surowiecki wrote in his bestselling book, *The Wisdom of Crowds*, Galton had stumbled on "the simple but powerful truth that . . . under the right circumstances, groups are remarkably intelligent, and are often smarter than the smartest people in them." This turns out to work for guessing gumballs and finding the coordinates of lost submarines, as well as determining the weight of butchered oxen. As Surowiecki went on to detail, drawing on the work of cognitive scientists, economists, and others, there are more such circumstances than one would have imagined. *And that's Keinan's solution.*

He read Surowiecki at the Harvard Business School and theorized that we must tap into the wisdom of the Jewish crowd to provide "a model of Judaism compelling enough that the vast majority of Jews, in America and Israel, will embrace it willingly." This, oddly, is more or less what he thinks Rabbi Yehuda ha-Nasi was doing in the third century when he codified the Mishnah. But the ancient Rabbis were intellectual elitists who disdained the crowd. Their ideal system of governance could be called a representative meritocracy, run by jurists who valued precedent highly even when they departed from it. To the extent that it was a democracy, it was, to employ Chesterton's famous phrase, "a democracy of the dead."

Nonetheless, Keinan finds it "difficult to ignore the neatness of the theory that Crowd Wisdom served as Diaspora Jewry's method of governance," and he thinks he sees Surowiecki's three criteria for wise crowds working through Jewish history.

> Dispersion created . . . *independence.* Communities in the Russian Pale, for example, were cut off from the ghettoes of Western Europe. . . . Each interpreted its Talmud independently. . . .
>
> Jewish communities in the Diaspora were culturally diverse. Bankers in the Venetian ghetto were affected by their interactions with the Venetian business community . . . making their experiences distinct from Ottoman Jews. . . . [They] formed a mosaic of *diversity.*
>
> Periodic migrations and expulsions over the centuries forced the *aggregation* and reconciliation of ideas that had diverged in isolation. The simple average that we used to aggregate guesses at the number of gumballs in a jar was an unsophisticated operation. This qualitative Jewish reconciliation would have been far more complex, but it served the same function.

Real history is not so neat. The ghettoes of Western Europe were largely gone by the time of the Russian Pale (that's the beginning of the story of Emancipation and assimilation, and Keinan is grappling with their effects); Shylock certainly had distinct experiences from Rabbi Joseph Karo, but what of it? And though migrations and expulsions do mark the medieval and early modern Jewish experience, a strong web of scholarly, business, and personal ties always connected Jewish communities. When Maimonides answered the questions of the Jews of Southern France from his twelfth-century home in Cairo, their exchange was certainly "far more complex" than counting gumballs, but it did not, even remotely, "serve the same function." In his zeal, Keinan seems to have forgotten that both the miracle and the limitation of crowd wisdom is that there is spontaneous coordination without conversation. It works for markets, but tradition and the scholarship that sustains it are not a market function.

Nonetheless, Keinan suggests that the "evolving Jewish moral code" is like a "moving stock average of more than three thousand years of religious, cultural, and moral data points." But charting a moving average to eliminate "noise" and smooth the trend line presupposes that the data points are just that: points on an x/y graph. But how does one graph, to take a simple case, a biblical verse through its various commentaries and literary uses? The ungraphable details matter; one might even say that God is in them (and not in the graphable crowd).

THE CLIMAX OF THE BOOK is Keinan's description of a closed-door Israeli Air Force meeting after a 2002 attack on a Hamas terrorist in Gaza whose operations had killed hundreds of Israelis. The terrorist, Salah Shehade, was killed, but so were civilians. Israeli Air Force commander Dan Halutz led the meeting, which Keinan describes as turning quickly from a tactical debriefing to an impassioned moral discussion. It ended without consensus (twenty-seven pilots later publicly resigned), but all voices were heard. "We knew," he writes, "we would never have perfect answers, but through some invisible cognition, the community's combined struggle for an answer had come close . . . This is how Diaspora had worked."

This may or may not have much to do with how the diaspora worked, but it has nothing to do with strangers counting gumballs or a market achieving equilibrium. A town-hall meeting like this might be better described in Hirschman's terms: Keinan and his fellow fighter pilots had (like American Jews) three options: loyalty, exit, or voice.

Unfortunately, Keinan's proposal for the revitalization of Jewish life is high-tech gumball counting:

> Imagine a machine designed . . . for applying the wisdom of a large crowd. . . . This machine's inputs would consist of the textual opinions, insights, predictions, and prescriptions of the subject community. The machine would rank the input . . . by means of an objective logic. . . . It would continually aggregate and reconcile these inputs into a constantly evolving Crowd Wisdom.

The problem with this is not the sci-fi conceit or even its sheer incoherence—how exactly does one teach one's children "constantly evolving Crowd Wisdom," and why?—but rather the premise that if we just had good enough data on what most Jews think Judaism should be, to the extent that they have thought about it at all, then that's what it should be.

In the absence of a "wisdom machine," Keinan ran a poll of various Jewish acquaintances asking them to list ten identifiers that "form the de facto pillars of contemporary Jewish identity." The top five results were justice, education, challenge and dissent, ritual and tradition, and community (neither God nor Torah made the list). On this basis, he proposes a world Jewish tax that would fund summer camps, a high-school *tikkun olam* project, and college tuition for all participating Jews (has he heard about Jewish life on American college campuses?). In other words, more of the same at the cost of, he estimates, $13.75 billion.

It's a shame, really, because there are parts of a better, more thoughtful book lurking in this sleek bestseller. They can be found in the passages in which Keinan charts his own fascinating Jewish journey and takes with ultimate seriousness the idea that both Israeli and American Jewry need a fundamental reorientation. As he writes in the final sentence of the book, "If Rabbi Yehuda, and all the successive generations that preserved our fragile legacy for so long, could ask us one question, perhaps it should be: *Who are you to end it?*"

II

Liberal and Illiberal Arts

A Party in Boisk

ON TUESDAY, the fifth of Nisan, 1843, in the town of Boisk, a little way outside of Riga, the *Hevrat Aggadeta*, a society for the study of Talmudic legends, had a party:

> We rejoiced in the joy of the commandment [*simcha shel mitzvah*] that God had helped us to study and to teach and to finish the Aggadeta . . . We celebrated for two whole days. On Tuesday we finished . . . and we made a party, a joyous occasion and a festival day. We invited 123 guests, not counting the musicians and the 15 waiters. There were four fancy courses, and [there was so much food that] every plate had at least a little left over, so that if a man hadn't eaten in three days he would have been satisfied and full . . . Our joy was an exceedingly great one in the joyousness of the mitzvah. We poured the wine like it was water—some pouring it down their throats and others on the floor.

Then, like Chuck Berry, they decided to do it again:

> On Wednesday, we began anew the study of the Aggadeta, and we took upon ourselves the obligation to learn and

to teach the books of the *Ein Ya'akov*. So we made another great feast to rejoice yet again in the joy of the mitzvah. And all the people made merry with trumpets and fiddles, and the earth split with the noise. And the people who stood outside and saw our joyousness envied us the joy of the mitzvah.

I teach at a liberal arts college, and I've never seen a Bloomsday at which undergrads gloried like this in the completion of *Ulysses*. The difference, of course, is in that recurring phrase *simcha shel mitzvah*, the joy of the commandment, but the boisterous, bodily joy these Boiskers took in fulfilling the commandment to study Torah is still surprising—and that may have something to do with the Torah they chose to study. To be brief, it was the lore, not the law. In fact, it is easy to imagine that the envious people "who stood outside and saw our joyousness," were actually Talmudic elitists, who looked down upon the elation of these ordinary Jews—workers, tradesmen, shopkeepers— at having finished a bunch of stories. "Well, we showed *them* what real *simcha shel mitzvah* was," one imagines the members of the society saying.

The work that the members of the *Hevrat Aggadeta* rejoiced in concluding and committed themselves to re-reading is a curious set of books. In the early 1500s a scholar named Ya'akov ibn Habib, who had been expelled from Spain in 1492 and then from Portugal five years later, found himself in the Ottoman city of Salonica with access to the great library of the famous Benveniste family. There he had a radical literary idea. The Babylonian Talmud had often been stripped, in one way or another, of its anecdotes, legends, myths, folk wisdom, jokes, and sermons, leaving only the halakha, the law unadorned. This is what Rabbi Yitzhak Alfasi had done in his classic *Sefer ha-Halakhot*, which was the basis for all of the halakhic codes of the Middle Ages.

What if one did precisely the opposite and kept only the aggada?

In her study of Ibn Habib, Marjorie Lehman argues that he intended his *Ein Ya'akov* (Well of Jacob) to be a source of religious faith for a community that needed it after years of forced conversions (including that of his son) and exile. Lehman makes a strong case for the project as an attempt to bolster the faith of a traumatized Sephardic community. But I wouldn't underestimate aesthetic joy as a motive.

The bitterness of exile and the bright glitter of literary beauty come together in the brilliant first lines of Ibn Habib's introduction. All of the *midrashim*, he says, are lost, "scattered" about the Talmud, where they shine like stars in a luminous firmament. The *Ein Ya'akov*, then, is a literary ingathering, beginning with Rabban Gamliel waiting impatiently for his sons to get back from a late-night party through everything from the famous stories of Rabbi Akiva's marriage and Elisha ben Abuya's apostasy to Pinchas ben Yair's remarkable donkey, God's comportment in the heavenly academy, and on and on, until it closes with a mishnah, in which Rabbi Yehoshua ben Levi promises the righteous "310 worlds" in the afterlife, based on a fanciful reading of a verse in Proverbs.

Some fifty years after the *Hevrat Aggadeta*'s big party, a young Abraham Isaac Kook took the job as the rabbi of Boisk. He had studied at the yeshiva of Volozhin, where there was a controversy between those who thought that the curriculum should be largely devoted to the study of the Talmud in its legal, halakhic aspect and those who wanted to supplement such study with an intense regimen of spiritual self-reflection (or even castigation), known as mussar. I don't know if the *Hevrat Aggadeta* was still active in the 1890s, but in Boisk Rav Kook began writing a commentary to the *Ein Ya'akov*. Yehudah Mirsky, his leading biographer, describes it as an attempt to show that the religious life was neither entirely a matter of halakha nor a perpetual battle with one's evil inclination, but rather "a lifelong effort at self-cultivation that would bring one's morals . . . into alignment with the divine ethos" that structures the universe.

Of course, the *Ein Ya'akov* was so popular because, whatever Ibn Habib's intentions or Rav Kook's interpretations, the carnival of its actual contents could never be contained under one tent, theological, ethical, or otherwise. Curiously, two of Rav Kook's fellow alumni from Volozhin, Chaim Nachman Bialik and Micha Yosef Berdichevsky, self-consciously compiled modern rivals to the *Ein Ya'akov*, both of which also attempted to make the aggada tell, as it were, a single story. Bialik's *Sefer Ha-Aggada* is elegant, classicizing, and compiled in the service of a secular-nationalist vision of Jewish tradition. Berdichevsky's various translations and anthologies are a raucous, Nietzschean attempt to rewrite the tradition from its own suppressed sources. (In one text he recovered, creation begins with the flatulence of Leviathan.)

I ran across the description of the party in Boisk in Simha Assaf's classic collection of primary sources on the history of Jewish education years ago. A generation younger than Kook, Assaf was another Lithuanian prodigy who, like Bialik and Kook, made aliyah. He eventually sat on the first Israeli Supreme Court as its halakhic expert.

There is a story about Assaf's arrival in Palestine as a young man, though, like most of the stories collected in the *Ein Yaakov*, it's probably apocryphal. Before Assaf went to present himself at one of the great *yeshivot*, a friend warned him not to boast that he knew "all of Shas," that is the entire Talmud, so he told the *rosh yeshiva* that he knew "half of Shas." "Which half?" the *rosh yeshiva* asked. "Which half do you want?" Assaf replied.

Solomon Schechter and the
Saint in the Drawing Room

SOMETIME AROUND 1903 the great scholar Solomon Schechter was provoked by a woman, whom he somewhat archly described as "a lady of the Jewish persuasion, of high culture and wide reading." She had remarked that

> Judaism is the only one among the great religions which has never produced a saint, and that there is, indeed, no room in it for that element of saintliness which, in other creeds, forms the goal the true believer endeavors to reach.

That, at least, is the conceit with which he opened his essay on "Saints and Saintliness," which was originally delivered as a public lecture at the Jewish Theological Seminary, where he had recently been recruited to be the president, and thus the intellectual leader of what would become Conservative Judaism.

Let us grant the conceit. After all, Schechter probably had such a conversation, if not in New York, then perhaps earlier in London or Cambridge. Whether it happened or

69

not, Schechter presents his interlocutor here as a social-intellectual type, a devotee of what he elsewhere calls the "shallow Enlightenment." The "great virtue" of her Judaism, Schechter went on to say, was "in its elasticity." It was

> adaptable to the latest result of the latest reconstruction of the Bible, and . . . compatible with any system of philosophy ever advanced,—provided of course that the system in question was the subject of languid conversation in fashionable drawing rooms.

In imagining Schechter's encounter with his "lady-friend," a little over a century ago, we must remember that he was not merely a learned scholar who occasionally found himself in fashionable drawing rooms. He was, despite his mastery of urbane late Victorian English prose, still Shlomo Zalman, the son of a ritual slaughterer (hence Schechter), a Lubavitcher hasid whom he once described as a "a saint."

In fact, Schechter not only described his father as a saintly, mild-mannered dreamer but said that his mother was "very quick-tempered," and that he took after his mother. The younger Schechter was well-known for his quick temper, and even his mature letters sometimes read more like dictated outbursts than the sober communications of a preeminent scholar and religious leader. Indeed, once one thinks about it, it is a little odd to begin an essay or lecture on "Saints and Saintliness," with a bit of condescending score-settling.

It seems to me there is also a deeper theological and historical ambivalence in Schechter's discussion of the topic. Modern "sane and plausible Judaism" was opposed to mysticism and enthusiasm, but, he acknowledged, "enthusiasm and mysticism are the very soil upon which saintliness survives best." And yet, while he clearly opposes his interlocutor's perfectly pliable and undemanding Judaism, and even says that "every religion wanting in Saints and Saintliness is doomed in the end to degenerate into commonplace virtues in action, and Philistinism in thought, [and] certain to disappear," neither does he advocate a return to the religious enthusiasm and mystical doctrines of his saintly subjects.

In his Introduction to the Second Series of his *Studies in Judaism*, Schechter remarked that "Saints and Saintliness" could be read as a companion to his earlier essay on the mystics of sixteenth-century Safed. The former, he wrote, "deals more with the thing 'saintliness,' 'Safed' [the essay] treats more of saints." In fact, Schechter took up these topics repeatedly in his writings.

SCHECHTER TAKES as the best Hebrew equivalent of saint the term Hasid, which, he quickly stipulates should not be taken as referring to "organisations or societies bearing that name." What distinguishes the Hasid more or less throughout Jewish history is, he says, a kind of spiritual individualism:

> The golden mean, so much praised by the philosophers and teachers of ethics, has no existence for him, and he is rather inclined to excesses. Nor can he be measured by the standard of the Law, for it is one of the characteristics of the saint that he never waits for a distinctive commandment.

Schechter admits that, if this is the case, "our theme would be best treated by a series of monographs," on saintly individuals, but proposes instead to sketch a kind of ideal type analysis, which better fits the scope of an essay. Here Schechter does something rhetorically remarkable and biographically interesting, though it only becomes truly evident in his footnotes, and has—as far as I know—never been remarked upon.

He begins by defining saintliness as "the effect of a religious experience when man enters into a close communion with Divine." In doing so, Schechter cites a rabbinic dictum and paraphrases "some New England mystic," who wrote of "the mingling of the individual soul with the universal soul." Schechter might have expected his cultured American audience to catch his coy allusion to Emerson, but his failure to speak about the recent and ongoing phenomenon of Eastern European Hasidism more directly is striking, even, perhaps, biographically revealing. For while he has already obliquely specified that those "organizations and societies" that use the term "hasid" are not his subject, he also immediately goes on to speak about the way in which the saint's desire for mingling with the universal soul exceeds the set times for prayer, without ever mentioning that this was a unique and controversial aspect of the early Hasidic movement. Indeed, the question of *unio mystica*, or *devekut*, was, and remains, central to the Lubavitcher Hasidism in which Schechter was raised.

Moreover, as the essay progresses, it becomes clear from his footnotes that Schechter's principal models for the ideal-type Saint/Hasid are, in fact, the great figures of nineteenth-century Hasidism. Thus, even when citing biblical or rabbinic or medieval sources in this context, he tends to quote those especially favored in the Hasidic tradition. For this "general sketch" Schechter favors the acts, sayings, and teachings from Pinchas of Koretz, Rabbi Mordechai of Chernobyl, and Rabbi Nachman of Bratzlav—all disciples of Baal Shem Tov.

The longest quoted text in Schechter's essay is from the *Igeret Ha-Kodesh* by the founder of Lubavitch Hasidism, Rabbi Shneur Zalman of Liadi, whom Schecter describes simply as "a well-known saint in Russia." Towards the end of the essay Schechter adduces this long text, of which I will quote only a small extract, to show the way in which the god-intoxicated Hasid "transgresses" the halakhic limits on charity in his care for the poor:

> My beloved ones . . . I have no doubt about the distress of the time. . . . . It is true that the law teaches that man's own life comes first, but this is only to be applied to things on which life depends . . . but if it is a question of bread and clothes and wood on one side, and dinners with fish and meat and fruit on the other side, the latter have to be given up as things superfluous. First the poor must be provided for with the necessaries of life. . . .

Then, for the first time, Schechter alludes to the mystical doctrines underlying Rabbi Shneur Zalman's thought as well as that of many of the figures whose actions and teachings he has been discussing. Rabbi Shneur Zalman, he says, "proceeds, in a long, mystical discourse, to show how the grace of heaven can be encouraged to flow into the proper channels, as the term is, only by manifestations of grace on earth."

Schechter's brief and metaphysically vague description of late Kabbalistic doctrine with regard to earthly action and supernal Sefirot returns us to our point of departure. As Schechter stood in that "languid drawing room," being told by "a Jewish woman of wide culture and reading" that Judaism was so sane that it had no saints, we must imagine him thinking of the Hasidic world he had left, which, for all its faults, had revolved around true saints who had, at least for a while, survived and even thrived on the "soil of enthusiasm and mysticism."

No doubt Schechter saw himself, the Jewish Theological Seminary, and the moderate traditionalism he represented as standing between the triumphant liberalism of the drawing room and the mystical enthusiasm of the Hasidic *shtiebl*. In the essay provoked by his drawing room conversation, Schechter wrote that "every religion wanting in the necessary sprinkling of Saints and Saintliness is doomed in the end." But on what metaphysical and spiritual soil did he think future saints of his own party of Judaism would survive?

The Chabad Paradox

THE HASIDIC GROUP known both as Lubavitch, after a town in Russia, and as Chabad, an acronym for the three elements of human and divine intelligence, *Chochma* (wisdom), *Bina* (understanding), and *Da'at* (knowledge), is not just the most successful contemporary Hasidic sect. It might be the most successful Jewish religious movement of the second half of the twentieth century.

While mainstream Orthodox Judaism has seen extraordinary growth through the *ba'al teshuvah* movement of "returners" to religious observance, the foundations were laid by Chabad. And while Orthodox Jews often express disdain for Chabad and its fervent *shluchim* (emissaries), they also rely on them for prayer services, Torah study, and kosher accommodations in out-of-the-way places—from Jackson, Wyoming, to Bangkok, Thailand, not to speak of college campuses around the world.

The Conservative movement historically caters to moderate suburban traditionalists. But many suburbanites now find themselves more comfortable at Chabad's user-friendly services. Once the source of a distinctive middle-class Jewish nightmare—that one's child might come home with *tzitzis*, a fedora, and extraordinary dietary demands (an "invasion of the Chabody snatchers," as a joke of my childhood had it)—Lubavitch is now a familiar part of the suburban landscape.

For decades, the Reform movement has defined its mission as *tikkun olam*, "repair of the world," understood not as metaphysical doctrine but as social justice. And yet it is the unabashedly metaphysical Chabad that opens drug rehabilitation centers, establishes programs for children with special needs, and caters to Jewish immigrants, to name just three of a seemingly endless list of charitable activities.

Finally, the charismatic founders of the groovy Judaism that arose in the 1960s, from the liberal Renewal movement to Neo-Hasidic Orthodoxy, were Rabbis Shlomo Carlebach and Zalman Schachter-Shalomi. Both began their careers as *shluchim* of the sixth Lubavitcher Rebbe in the late 1940s and continued under his successor before branching out on their own. Although neither remained within Chabad, both retained its can-do entrepreneurial flair, as well as a spark, as it were, of the Rebbe's charisma.

Each of these points needs qualification, but each could also be amplified. Despite its tiny numbers—at a generous guess, Lubavitchers have never comprised more than one percent of the total Jewish population—the Chabad-Lubavitch movement has transformed the Jewish world. It also has enviable brand recognition. This extends from the distinctive black suits, untrimmed beards, and genuine warmth of Chabad *shluchim* to renegade but still recognizably Chabad-ish figures like the reggae pop star Matisyahu and religious pundit Shmuley Boteach. But, most of all, Chabad is recognized in the saintly and ubiquitous visage of the late seventh Lubavitcher Rebbe, Menachem Mendel Schneerson, which has become, almost literally, a kind of icon.

By almost any conceivable standard, Chabad-Lubavitch has been an extraordinary success, except by the one standard that it has set itself: It has not ushered in the Messiah. It has, however, been the source of the greatest surge of Jewish messianic fervor ("We want Moshiach now and we don't want to wait!") since the career of Shabbtai Tzvi, the failed messiah of the seventeenth century. In fact, there are an indeterminate number of messianist Lubavitchers (*meshikhistn*) who continue to believe that the Rebbe did not truly die in 1994, and will return to complete his messianic mission. This is repudiated by the central organization of Chabad, though not as unequivocally as some critics would like. In any case, a successor to Schneerson seems inconceivable even to such apparent moderates within the movement.

This raises a large question. It is often said of Chabad that the success of its institution-building and good works are unfortunately marred by its ardent messianism. But what if this messianism was the motivating force that actually made their success possible? If so, we would be presented with a kind of paradox: the belief that underlies the Lubavitchers' success may yet undo them entirely.

CERTAINLY, NONE of Chabad's successes would have been likely or even possible had the movement not been headed, since 1951, by Rabbi Schneerson, the subject of sociologists Samuel Heilman and Menachem Friedman's ambitious and already controversial new biography, *The Rebbe: The Life and Afterlife of Menachem Mendel Schneerson.*

Schneerson was born in 1902 in Ukraine to a distinguished Lubavitcher family. Heilman and Friedman sketch his early life, but their most striking biographical claims come in the chapters on his young adult years. It used to be said that in the 1920s and 1930s, Schneerson had received degrees from the University of Berlin and the Sorbonne.

Actually, Friedman and Heilman show that when Schneerson left Russia for Germany he did not have a diploma and so was unable to seek regular admission to a university. Instead, he applied to audit courses at the neo-Orthodox Hildesheimer Rabbinical Seminary, which in turn allowed him to audit courses at Friedrich Wilhelm University. Later, in Paris, he received an engineering degree from the École Spéciale des Travaux Publics du Bâtiment et de l'Industrie, and went on to study mathematics at the Sorbonne before being forced to flee the occupying Nazis.

It was while auditing courses in philosophy and mathematics in Berlin that Schneerson married Moussia (or Chaya Mushka), the daughter of Rabbi Yosef Yitzchak Schneersohn, the sixth Lubavitcher Rebbe (the bride and groom were distantly related). Here Heilman and Friedman strive mightily to show that, far from being destined to succeed his father-in-law as Rebbe, Menachem Mendel and his new wife were trying out a less Hasidic, more cosmopolitan lifestyle. They write that "visitors of the few Hasidic congregations" in Berlin never saw Schneerson in attendance, and that he and Moussia liked to go out on the town on Monday nights. They also scant his Jewish study, and, almost as provocatively, strongly suggest that he trimmed his beard. In these chapters, Schneerson is described as leading a "double life."

This is interesting, and may be true in some sense, but it would be more persuasive if Heilman and Friedman really had the goods. When one checks the endnote for who didn't see Menachem Mendel Schneerson in shul, the only name turns out to be that of Yosef Burg. In the 1980s, the prominent Israeli politician told Friedman that he did not remember seeing Schneerson—a half century after the fact. What about those nights out in Weimar-era Berlin? They are mentioned on the authority of the "recollections of Barry Gourary," a nephew who was then five years old, lived in Latvia at the time, and later became bitterly estranged from his aunt and uncle.

The question of Schneerson's rabbinic learning, his beard, and the couple's years in Berlin and Paris have been the subject of a furious dispute between Samuel Heilman and a clever Chabad blogger named Chaim Rapoport on a popular Orthodox website, *Seforim*. Although somewhat self-righteous and bombastic, Rapoport has gotten the better of the exchange. Even in Heilman and Friedman's account, for instance, it emerges that during the period when Schneerson is supposed to have avoided Hasidic *shtiblekh*, he was piously fasting every day until the afternoon. Heilman and Friedman hypothesize that this was because he and Moussia were childless, but, as Rapoport points out, he began the practice immediately after marriage. The fact that the Schneersons never had children is of extraordinary biographical and historical importance (if they had, the possibility of an eighth Lubavitcher Rebbe might have seemed more thinkable), but Schneerson would have had to be a prophet to begin worrying about this in 1929.

More importantly, Rapoport shows that remarks such as "a look through [Schneerson's] diary . . . reveals that he had been collecting and absorbing the myriad customs of Lubavitcher practice for years" seriously understate the extent of Schneerson's learning and piety. Schneerson's posthumously published diary, *Reshimot*, along with his learned correspondence with his father and father-in-law, present a picture of someone thoroughly engaged in the intellectual worlds of rabbinic thought, Kabbalah, and Hasidism. Occasionally, one even finds him working to integrate all of this with his scientific studies. In one such entry, he links the fluidity of one's inner experience to the traditional comparison of Torah with water, as well as to Pascal's law of hydrostatic pressure.

This is hardly to deny that Schneerson contemplated leading a life devoted to engineering and science rather than religious leadership; the years of difficult schooling are inexplicable otherwise. But it is a failure of biographical research and imagination on Heilman and Friedman's part not to have critically culled Schneerson's correspondence and journals to give a sense of his inner life in all of its fluidity. He was an aspiring engineer and a kabbalist, but since Heilman and Friedman take an extremely selective approach to the letters and journals of this period of his life, they fail to portray the second half of the equation. In part, this is because the sources were edited within a Chabad movement zealously dedicated to the memory of its Rebbe, so Friedman and Heilman are not wrong to approach them with skepticism, but it plainly also has to do with the difficulty of the material, with its cryptic hints at kabbalistic doctrine and rabbinic practice.

Their circumstantial approach to biography reaches its height, or depth, in Heilman and Friedman's account of the Schneersons' years in Paris. The couple chose to live in the fourteenth *arrondissement*, far from synagogues but just moments from the café Le Select, where "one could find the most outrageous bohemian behavior," and within hailing distance of some of Sartre and Beauvoir's favorite haunts. "Could the Schneersons have remained completely ignorant of this life around them?" Heilman and Friedman ask. Based on the evidence presented, my guess would be mostly yes. (One *would* like to know more about Moussia, who read Russian literature and attended the ballet, but she remains a cipher throughout the book, as does the Schneersons' marital relationship.)

As for whether Schneerson cut his beard as a young man, I remain agnostic, if not indifferent. A photograph from the period shows a dapper Schneerson in a brown suit, light-colored hat, and short beard, standing on a bridge and looking out at the water. But Lubavitchers sometimes comb their beards under and pin them to achieve a neat look. Heilman and Friedman hedge by describing the beard as "trim-looking," but they clearly think scissors were involved and that his father-in-law was furious. Yet in pictures taken two decades later, after he had already become the Rebbe, Schneerson still looks well-groomed. In one, he stares back at the camera, his eyes framed by a sharp black hat and a trim black beard, looking a little like a rabbinic Paul Muni.

LIVES OF SAINTS have a sense of fatedness or inevitability that Heilman and Friedman are certainly right to avoid. Menachem Mendel Schneerson was not predestined to become the seventh Rebbe, let alone the Messiah, except in the much later hagiographic stories told about him by his followers.

In fact, there was significant opposition to his succeeding his father-in-law. In the first place, there was his mother-in-law. Nechama Dina Schneersohn favored her other son-in-law, Rabbi Shmaryahu Gourary (the above-mentioned Barry's father), who had been at her husband's side while Schneerson was studying in Berlin and Paris. Schneerson's ascension was not immediate, and his eventual victory left a deeply divided family. Symbolically, his mother-in-law refused to allow him to wear her husband's *shtrayml*, the fur hat worn on Shabbat, Holy Days, and important occasions. Heilman and Friedman describe Schneerson's pragmatic response with a rare sense of admiration:

> Rabbi Menachem Mendel handled this as he handled other challenges, with creativity. He simply removed the use of *shtraymls* from Chabad rabbinic practice and

was forever after seen only in his trademark black snap brim fedora.

Schneerson was clearly an inspired tactician and executive, with a genius for public relations. Again and again, Heilman and Friedman show, he was able to inspire and empower his followers to spread the message to perform more ritual commandments and acts of loving-kindness. But they also see early signs of Messianic ambition.

Near the end of his great twelfth-century code of Jewish law, the *Mishneh Torah*, Maimonides lays out the criteria for the true Messiah:

> If a king arises from the House of David who delves deeply into the study of the Torah . . . if he compels all Israel to walk in [its ways] . . . and fights the wars of God, he is presumed to be the Messiah. If he succeeds and builds the Holy Temple on its site and gathers the scattered remnants of Israel, then he is certainly the Messiah.

If one identifies the "kingship" of Lubavitch with that of the House of David, then the Rebbe's missionary work through his many public campaigns—to encourage the lighting of Shabbat candles, the wearing of *tefillin*, and so on—can be seen as steps toward fulfilling Maimonides' second criterion. And what of "the wars of God"? The Chabad youth group *Tzivos Hashem*, or the "Army of God," was established under the leadership of a Rebbe who also dispatched "mitzvah tanks" emblazoned with inspirational slogans. More speculatively, Heilman and Friedman also argue that the Rebbe competed with the State of Israel by taking spiritual credit for its military victories. In short, the overarching goal of Chabad's activities was to make the Rebbe the presumptive Messiah and "force the end" of history, to use a classic (and disparaging) Rabbinic phrase.

Certainly, this is how many if not most of his Hasidim seem to have understood these activities at the time. Although he often rebuked those who publicly urged him to declare his Messianic kingship, what they took him to mean was "not yet." They were probably right. Chabad doctrine holds that there is a potential savior in every generation, and it seems unlikely that Schneerson thought that it was somebody else. Friedman and Heilman say that he hinted at this when he used the Hebrew word *mamash*. The word means "really," or "actually," but it can also be taken as an acronym for the name Menachem Mendel Schneerson. Thus, on the occasion of being honored by President Ronald Reagan the Rebbe said that the "Messiah is coming soon, *mamash*," and he is reported to have later repeated the assurance, adding "with all its interpretations."

The parsing of such hints and proclamations may sound trivial, but the radical seriousness with which Schneerson and his followers took their spiritual task should not be underestimated. He really does seem to have felt responsible for all Jews and to have conveyed a sense of this deep caring to virtually each of the thousands who sought an individual audience, or "yechidus," with him. His followers took this same sense of care to the streets and around the world, and continue to do so.

Schneerson's charisma was palpable even to non-followers. Norman Mailer, a connoisseur of charisma if not of theology, felt it when he and Norman Podhoretz visited Chabad headquarters at 770 Eastern Parkway for *kol nidrei* in 1962. The willingness of non-Hasidim to tell miraculous tales of the Rebbe also suggests an extraordinary personality that is sadly not on display in *The Rebbe*. Even if he was not the Messiah, the Rebbe may have been the most influential Hasidic leader since Israel Ba'al Shem Tov, the founder of the movement. Heilman and Friedman's biography simply doesn't show us how Schneerson became that person.

THE REBBE does show that the messianism, which burst into public awareness in the 1970s and '80s, was present from the outset of Schneerson's leadership, and had its roots in his father-in-law's understanding of Hasidism.

In 1751, the Ba'al Shem Tov described a vision in which he ascended to heaven:

> I entered the palace of the Messiah, where he studies with all the Rabbinic sages and the righteous . . . I asked, "when are you coming, sir?" He answered me: ". . . [not] until your teaching has become renowned and revealed throughout the whole world. . . ." I was bewildered at this [and] I had great anguish because of the length of time when it would be possible for this to occur.

Gershom Scholem, the great historian of Jewish mysticism, saw this postponement as evidence that Hasidism was, in part, an attempt to neutralize the kabbalistic messianism of Shabbtai Tzvi and his followers while retaining its popular dynamism. His interpretation has been the subject of much scholarly controversy, but it fits the *Tanya*, the first work of Chabad Hasidism, by its founder Schneur Zalman of Liadi. The "Alter Rebbe," as he is known within Chabad, describes messianic redemption as the final illumination of the revelation begun at Sinai, but it does not sound imminent.

However, by Rabbi Yosef Yitzchak Schneersohn's reign there had been seven generations of Hasidic Rebbes who had followed the Ba'al Shem Tov, and six generations of Lubavitcher Rebbes. As early as 1926, Yosef Yitzchak emphasized the importance of a midrashic statement that "all sevens are dear to God," suggesting that the seventh generation might inaugurate the messianic period, the final Sabbath of history. In the 1940s, after experiencing the depredations of Communist rule and seeing some of his family and much of his world destroyed by the Nazis, he coined the slogan *le-alter le-teshuvah, le-alter le-geulah* ("repentance now, redemption now").

Rabbi Yosef Yitzchak's last work was entitled *Basi Legani*, or "I have come into my garden," after the biblical verse, "I have come into my garden, my sister, my bride" (Song of Songs 5:1), traditionally understood as a poetic allegory of the consummation of the love between God and Israel, and also that between God and his exiled (feminine) presence, the *Shekhina*. It was delivered posthumously by Schneerson on the anniversary of his father-in-law's passing, in what was to become his first address as Rebbe. Schneerson consoled his father-in-law's Hasidim and himself by emphasizing that "the seventh is cherished." Just as Moses and his generation had followed Abraham by seven generations, so too this generation was now the seventh Hasidic generation, whose task was to complete the process of drawing down the *Shekhina*. The end of the address is worth quoting at some length.

This accords with what is written concerning the Messiah: "And he shall be exalted greatly . . ." even more than was Adam before the sin. And my revered father-in-law, the Rebbe, of blessed memory . . . who was "anguished by our sins and ground down by our transgressions,"— *just as he saw us in our affliction, so will he speedily in our days . . . redeem the sheep of his flock simultaneously from both the spiritual and physical exile, and uplift us to [a state where we shall be suffused with] rays of light* . . . Beyond this, the Rebbe will bind and unite us with the infinite Essence of God . . . "Then will Moses and the Children of Israel sing . . . 'God will reign forever and ever,' " . . . All the above is accomplished through the passing of tzaddikim, which is even harsher than the destruction of the Temple. Since we have already experienced all these things, everything now depends only on us—the seventh generation. *May we be privileged to see and meet with the Rebbe here in this world, in a physical body, in this earthly domain—and he will redeem us.*

Heilman and Friedman (who don't discuss the discourse in its entirety) understand Schneerson to have been asserting from the very beginning that as the seventh Lubavitcher Rebbe he was destined to be the Messiah. But perhaps we ought to take him at his word here. In the sentences I have italicized, he is clearly describing his father-in-law as the Messiah who will "speedily in our days . . . redeem the sheep of his flock," and will do so, moreover, "in a physical body, in this earthly domain." So, who was the beloved "seventh"? Schneerson may have been saying that it was his father-in-law—counting seven generations after the Ba'al Shem Tov and either placing himself as a mere member of that seventh generation under his father-in-law, or, perhaps, merging himself with his father-in-law as he does in the text. This is personally more modest but theologically bolder than the alternative, for it already sets the precedent for one of the features of present-day Lubavitcher messianism that many find so objectionable: the promise that a Messiah who has died will return a second time to complete the redemption.

Schneerson continued to elaborate on the themes of *Basi Legani* every year on his father-in-law's *yahrzeit*. It would be interesting to see if and how the interpretation evolved, but Heilman and Friedman have little time for textual analysis of any kind. Unfortunately, this is a biography of an intellectual (Schneerson was immersed in the reading and writing of abstruse texts throughout his life) that shows little interest in its subject's intellectual biography.

WHAT DID SCHNEERSON think the Messianic era would look like? Elliot Wolfson's recent book, *Open Secret: Postmessianic Messianism and the Mystical Revision of Menahem Mendel Schneerson*, provides an astonishing answer. Wolfson, who is one of the leading scholars of Jewish mysticism of his generation, has little interest in court politics or the externals of Schneerson's biography, but he has read his mystical writings very closely. This is not easy work. Not only did the Rebbe write an extraordinary amount (the collected Hebrew and Yiddish discourses alone comprise thirty-nine volumes), but he wrote in a rebarbative style that goes all the way back to the *Tanya*. The historian Joseph Weiss once described it as "marked by long sentences, extremely condensed in character, with the main subordinate clauses often mixed up, and frequent anacoluthic constructions." This sounds about right, as long as one adds the penchant for deliberate paradox, though there are also sudden moments of beauty.

Wolfson is a difficult writer himself, but he has read the Rebbe with extraordinary sympathy and erudition. To explain the notion of primordial essence in Chabad metaphysics, he cites "Schelling's notion of 'the absolute indifference' of the being or essence (*Wesen*) that precedes all ground and is thus referred to as the 'original ground,' the *Ungrund*, literally the *nonground*," which is to say that it is something like Aristotle's prime matter, which becomes all things without being anything specific in itself. On Wolfson's reading of Schneerson, in the Messianic era all differences—those between man and woman, Jew and gentile (though Schneerson was not as consistent as he would like here) and even God and the universe—will be returned to something like the original nonground of Schellingian indifference.

And how will the Messiah do this? Wolfson's interpretation is an act of hermeneutic chutzpah:

> In my judgment, Schneerson was intentionally ambiguous about his own identity as Messiah . . . Simply put, the image of the personal Messiah may have been utilized rhetorically to liberate one from the belief in the personal Messiah . . . Schneerson's mission from its inception is about fostering the "true expansion of knowledge" . . . an alternate angle of vision . . . marked by progressively discarding all veils in the effort to see the veil of truth unveiled in the truth of the veil.

The king, as it were, has paraded without clothes in order to show that there is no difference between being clothed and naked, or as Kafka said, "the Messiah will come only when he is no longer necessary." This is clever, in a postmodern humanities seminar kind of way, but if Schneerson was really trying to liberate his followers from their belief in a personal messiah, one must say that he did a spectacularly bad job of it.

IN 1991, A FRAIL eighty-nine-year-old Rebbe addressed his Hasidim poignantly:

> What more can I do? I have done all I can so that the Jewish people will demand and clamor for the redemption, for all that was done up to now was not enough, and the proof is that we are still in exile and, more importantly, in internal exile from the worship of God. The only thing that remains for me to do is to give over the matter to you. Do all that is in your power to achieve this thing—a sublime and transcendent light that needs to be brought down into

our world with pragmatic tools—to bring the righteous Messiah, in fact immediately (*mamash miyad*).

I can see how to read this like Wolfson, but I can't buy it. The Rebbe, I believe, meant the Messiah *mamash*.

Gershom Scholem once described messianism as an anarchic breeze that throws the well-ordered house of Judaism into disarray. Although the official position of the Chabad movement is that Menachem Mendel Schneerson did in fact pass away and is not (or at least not so far) the Messiah, its house remains disordered. As I write, *yechi Adoneinu Morenu ve-Rabeinu Melekh ha-Moshiach le-olam va-ed* is chanted at prayer services in the Rebbe's own synagogue in the basement of Chabad headquarters. Their master and teacher and rabbi, the King Messiah, they proclaim, will live forever. Of course, the messianism extends beyond Crown Heights. My son has a handy card with the *tefillat ha-derekh*, the prayer for travelers on one side and a picture of the Rebbe over the word "Moshiach," which was thrust into his hands in Jerusalem. In recent months I have seen messianist banners, bumper stickers, posters and yarmulkes in Jerusalem, Tel Aviv, Los Angeles, Miami, and Cleveland.

To its great credit, Chabad's worldwide operations have continued to expand in the years since the Rebbe's death. But this fact does not quite undermine the paradox with which I began. Although many, perhaps most, within Chabad no longer live in an ecstatic anticipation of imminent redemption, the Rebbe still seems to be the mainspring for all of their activities. It is not just that there is no eighth Lubavitcher Rebbe and is not likely to be one until the Messiah comes (when, as Kafka might say, we will no longer need one), but that the fervent devotion to the previous Rebbe seems perilously close to crowding out other religious motivations.

Could Chabad continue to thrive if the seventh Lubavitcher Rebbe was no longer at the center of his followers' spiritual universe? If they came to see him in a light no different than that of his predecessors—a great leader but not the Messiah, a great rebbe but not irreplaceable? Can the apparently superhuman achievements of the Chabad movement continue if its Hasidim lose their superhuman inspiration?

Walter Benjamin, Gershom Scholem, and the Stones of Sinai

IN THE SUMMER of 1937, Gershom Scholem began planning his trip from Jerusalem to New York to deliver the lectures that would become his classic history, *Major Trends in Jewish Mysticism*. Among his first priorities—more pressing than visiting his mother or even the Bibliotheque Nationale—was arranging a meeting in Paris with Walter Benjamin, whom he had not seen in a decade.

Benjamin was not only his best friend, he was a thinker for whom Scholem held extraordinary, probably impossible hopes. Three years later, Scholem would dedicate *Major Trends* to Benjamin's memory, but that was an act of disappointment as well as of mourning.

Five years earlier, when Scholem had returned to Europe to treasure-hunt for Kabbalistic manuscripts (in Rome, Cambridge and Berlin), their plans for a meeting had misfired. Or perhaps Benjamin, who was at a loose end and depressed almost to the point of suicide, couldn't face his forceful, fanatically driven friend and deliberately scuttled the plans. "Oh, dear Gerhard," Benjamin wrote on February 28, 1932, "today I noticed to my horror that you are planning to leave on the twelfth and that your letter has been lying here for almost two months. . . ."

There had been another reason to avoid that meeting. The last time they had seen each other, Scholem had introduced Benjamin to Judah Magnes, the President of the Hebrew University. At Scholem's urging, Benjamin delivered an inspired account of how his philosophical reflections on translation, his study of Goethe and Hölderlin, and his interest in Judaism had led him to the conviction that he must immerse himself in the Hebrew language and its texts. He would, given the funding, go to Jerusalem, study Hebrew and become a Jewish philosopher-critic. Magnes was taken with Benjamin and authorized immediate payment for such a trip. However, despite year after year of desultory planning and promising, the closest Benjamin ever came to fulfilling his part of the deal was to hire a tutor and carry a Hebrew primer around Berlin for a couple of weeks. Scholem was furious. Not only had he wanted a Jerusalem reprise of their student days, in which he would now take the intellectual lead, he really believed that Benjamin could be the great Jewish philosopher-critic who would redeem fragments of lost Kabbalistic doctrine in a distinctively modern idiom. In these years Benjamin sometimes spoke as if he had in fact already done just that. He inscribed a copy of his first book, *The Origin of German Tragic Drama*, "to Gerhard Scholem, donated to the Ultima Thule of his Kabbalistic library."

To the end of his life, Scholem wondered at the inscription. Benjamin told Adorno and others that only someone who knew Kabbala could understand his book's "Epistemo-Critical Prologue." It should, however, be remembered that Benjamin was always a bluff artist. In Europe "Kabbala" had been a synonym for esoterica since at least the seventeenth century, and Ultima Thule was a medieval kingdom that never existed. In 1935, Scholem sent his friend a copy of his little book of translations from the Zohar, the medieval classic of Jewish mysticism. Benjamin responded, "There can be no question of my reading the book—with the exception of your foreword—from beginning to end," though he did go on to speak appreciatively of the Zohar's doctrine that words were "the deposits of cosmic connections." Benjamin took this idea from Scholem's first selected passage, on the creation of the world through divine language, an idea to which we shall return. The book itself was a little over 100 pages long.

Nonetheless, Benjamin's ideas of language as divine and history as containing the seeds of both apocalypse and redemption, his fondness for theological metaphors, and, of course, his deep friendship with Scholem have led many commentators on Benjamin to speculate on the Kabbalistic origins of his thought. Such speculations do not carry conviction. After all, Scholem was disappointed in Benjamin precisely because he had not really encountered premodern Jewish literary traditions. Benjamin scholars have sometimes been fooled by the resemblances between Scholem's accounts of Jewish mysticism (of which they have little first-hand knowledge) and Benjamin's ideas. But a better question is this: did Benjamin ever adapt an idea or image directly from a Jewish mystical text for his own distinctive purposes?

In the epistolary exchanges over Franz Kafka with which the two scholars patched up their friendship in the mid-1930s, Scholem repeatedly urged Benjamin to read Kafka's stories and parables in a Jewish theological light. For Scholem, they depicted a world in which revelation was absolutely necessary, but impossible, a kind of "secret law." In a long poem entitled "With a Copy of Kafka's Trial" and appended to a 1934 letter to Benjamin, he wrote:

> This is the sole ray of revelation in an age that disavowed you, entitled only to experience you in the shape of your negation.

Kafka's texts were, Scholem wrote elsewhere, "a secular statement of the Kabbalistic world-feeling in a modern spirit," and accordingly he gave seminars on *The Trial* to aspiring historians of religion at the Hebrew University. But Benjamin was the only critic whom he thought capable of producing a commentary worthy of Kafka's texts—if only he would stop sabotaging himself with hopeless love affairs, incoherent Communism, and endless dithering.

By 1937, none of their personal or intellectual differences had been resolved, but Benjamin and Scholem were nonetheless eager to see each other. After some haggling over the dates, they arranged to meet for a few days in February 1938, in Paris. It did not go well. Following the example of his new friend and mentor Bertolt Brecht, Benjamin refused to condemn, or even speak about, the Moscow show trials; Scholem hated Brecht's recent *Threepenny Novel* (a novelization of the opera), and was less than enthusiastic about Benjamin's new essay, "The Work of Art in the Age of Mechanical Reproduction." In his memoir, *Walter Benjamin: The Story of a Friendship*, Scholem wrote, "I attacked his use of the concept of aura which he had employed in an entirely different sense for many years and was now placing in what I considered a pseudo-Marxist context." Earlier, Benjamin had written of the aura as the unique, almost holy presence of an unreplicable work of art; now he was looking forward to its disappearance as a mystifying haze produced by bourgeois capitalism. And yet, there was also an elegiac tone to Benjamin's writing that still mourned this passing as the last remnant of cult and ritual. Scholem accused Benjamin of "sneaking in metaphysical insights into a framework unsuited to them," and argued (as have others since) that there was no compelling connection between his evocation of the aura and his idea of film as the proletarian art form of the future. Benjamin replied that "the Revolution" would show the connection between the two. Scholem, an anarcho-Zionist party of one, was not impressed.

He was even more upset by Benjamin's new ideas about language. They had once shared the metaphysical view that names, or at least true names, were to be distinguished from mere words, because they expressed the being of their bearers. In another now-celebrated essay, Benjamin had argued that this divine ur-language could be glimpsed in the act of translation from one language to another. Scholem found intimations of the same idea in Kabbalistic theories of revelation and the creative potency of the Hebrew language. But now Benjamin was insisting that language be demystified and understood as essentially political.

In his memoir, Scholem quotes Benjamin as saying, "I don't understand you. You were the one who so highly commended Scheerbart. . . . And now that I commend Brecht to your attention, who is completing what Scheerbart started— namely the writing of a totally unmagical language, a language cleansed of all magic—you show no interest!" Scholem replied that Scheerbart (a quirky Expressionist) had a sense of the infinite, to which Benjamin replied, "What matters is not infinity but the elimination of magic." Scholem protested. What about his friend's essays on language and translation, whose ideas were "developed further in the preface to his book on tragic drama"? Benjamin's recent essay "On the Mimetic Faculty" had tried to give some content to the idea that "every word . . . is onomatopoeic" with the mysterious idea that names and their referents shared a "non-sensuous similarity." Benjamin admitted the contradiction, but was unmoved.

At one point, he replied by reciting Brecht's sonnet "On Dante's Poems about Beatrice" to Scholem. In John Willett's translation of the published version, the first stanza reads:

> Even today, above the dusty vault
> In which she lies, whom he could never have
> Although he dogged her footsteps like a slave
> Her name's enough to bring us to a halt.

But Benjamin recited the unpublished version, in which the last word of the second line was not *haben* (have), but *ficken* (fuck). Forty years later, Scholem still remembered the unmagical shock of the moment. He spoke, Scholem wrote, "with perfect nonchalance, as though it contained the most commonly used word, but looking me full in the face while doing so." They came together again over Kafka and even discussed another scheme to get Benjamin to Jerusalem. After the visit, they continued to correspond; they also managed to miss each other on Scholem's return voyage. Two years later, Benjamin committed suicide at the French-Spanish border after the Spanish border police refused to accept his papers.

The next year, Scholem's *Major Trends in Jewish Mysticism* was published. Its dedication page reads, "To the memory of Walter Benjamin (1892–1940), the friend of a lifetime whose genius united the insight of the Metaphysician, the interpretive power of the Critic and the erudition of the Scholar. Died at Port Bou (Spain) on his way to freedom." Scholem's book was a work of imaginative, painstaking historical reconstruction, but it ended on an almost prophetic note. In the last paragraph, he wrote, "The story is not ended, it has not yet become history, and the secret life [Jewish mysticism] holds can break out tomorrow in you or in me." But there were only two people in whom Scholem really believed that the "Kabbalistic world-feeling" had broken out, or at least might have: Franz Kafka and Walter Benjamin.

In their Paris argument, Scholem had been right to point to the "Epistemo-Critical Prologue" to Benjamin's book *The Origin of German Tragic Drama*, as the most important source for the linguistic mysticism that he seemed then to be abandoning. As George Steiner writes, the book expresses "a Jewish hallowing of the word, an almost tactile sense of the mystery of saying." It was a book so idiosyncratic, densely brilliant, and obscure that when Benjamin submitted it as his *Habilitationsschrift*—the second book which was supposed to secure an academic position— at the University of Frankfurt, it ensured that he would never hold an academic position in Germany (though this became moot after 1933). In a key passage of the prologue, Benjamin wrote:

> In empirical perception, in which words have become fragmented, they possess, in addition to their more or less hidden, symbolic aspect, an obvious, profane meaning. It is the task of the philosopher to restore, by representation, the primacy of the symbolic character of the word, in which the idea is given self-consciousness, and that is the opposite of all outwardly-directed communication. Since philosophy may not presume to speak in the tones of revelation, this can only be achieved by recalling in memory the primordial form of perception. . . . Ultimately, however, this is not the attitude of Plato, but the attitude of Adam, the father of the human race and the father of philosophy. . . . Ideas are displayed, without intention, in the act of naming, and they have to be renewed in philosophical contemplation.

Benjamin was a murky, suggestive thinker whose work has often been misconstrued by readers too committed to turning him into a philosopher. Nonetheless, there is something like a doctrine, if not perhaps an argument, expressed here: the act of philosophical criticism (like the act of translation) has the potential to uncover the symbolic meanings of language in its primal form, in which it is made up entirely of true names: pure linguistic expressions of being. The philosophical contemplation that reveals this is the human counterpart to divine revelation, in whose tones we, at least, "may not presume to speak." In illustrating this idea, Benjamin did employ a Kabbalistic text, or at least what he thought was one.

Benjamin, who continually revised and rewrote the essays that were most important to him, had cut the passage from the final version. It is retained, however, in the valuable *Gesammelte Schriften*, edited by Rolf Tiedeman. There, Benjamin recounts a story about the stones at the foot of Mount Sinai: "(The stones) have impressed upon them the pattern of a . . . tree (the burning bush) whose peculiar nature consists in the fact that it reproduces itself immediately on every single piece of stone that has broken off from a stone block, and this into infinity." It is not impossible Benjamin had this missing passage in mind when he told Adorno that one would have to be a Kabbalist to understand his book, and when he wrote the tantalizing inscription on Scholem's copy. It is certainly the case that his earlier draft of the prologue was more forthrightly Jewish and theological in its concepts and concerns than the copy submitted to the faculty of the University of Frankfurt.

In any event, the image was deeply related to Benjamin's ideas of language and knowledge. As Ernst Bloch once noted, Benjamin proceeded "as if the world were language," and as if the only true language was divine. Moreover, in

The Origin of German Tragic Drama, he had elaborated a peculiarly idealistic theory of the origin of an idea or work of art. The true origin of an idea was, Benjamin taught, not to be identified with its historical emergence in some particular time and place, but rather with its essence as it might have been revealed at the moment of revelation or as it would be reestablished at the Messianic redemption. Looking back on the book a few years later, Benjamin wrote that his concept of the origin was really a "transposition" of Goethe's idea of Urphenomenon—of a biological archetype which replicates itself endlessly in the morphological structure of an organism—"from the realm of nature to that of history," and from the "pagan natural context" to the "Jewish historical context."

The image of the stones at Sinai was, then, an almost perfect expression of Benjamin's ideas, and perhaps as close as Benjamin got to fulfilling Scholem's hopes for him. For here we have Sinaitic revelation—the very origin of the "Jewish historical context"—in which divine language was supposed to have broken forth, literally impressing itself upon the world of the "pagan natural context," the world of stones. In doing so, it endlessly reproduces an archetypal image, in which each fragment carries with it both the aura and the full meaning of the original revelation. This image, moreover, of a tree or bush was one that Goethe, author of the *Metamorphosis of Plants*, would have particularly appreciated. Only it was not a myth.

In the most extensive scholarly discussion of this passage, Beatrice Hanssen has referred to it as a "Kabbalistic myth," though, as Hanssen knows, Benjamin did not learn this bit of homiletical arcana from Scholem or any other Kabbalist. Nor, of course, did it "break out" in some more mysterious way. Nothing from the past broke out in Benjamin or Scholem (or will break out in you or in me) that was not acquired somewhere. In this case, Benjamin read the story of the stones of Sinai in the popular eighteenth-century *Autobiography of Salomon Maimon*.

Maimon was an Eastern European Jew who in a characteristic act of chutzpa had renamed himself after his philosophical hero, the twelfth-century Jewish philosopher Moses Maimonides, author of the classic of medieval rationalism, *The Guide of the Perplexed*. In 1790, Maimon wrote a brilliant commentary on Kant's *Critique of Pure Reason*, which Kant himself praised ("none of my critics understood me and the main problems so well . . ."). Two years later Maimon wrote his autobiography, which was almost as personally frank as Rousseau's and, in some ways, even odder. Among its oddities was Maimon's decision to place a ten-chapter critical synopsis of Maimonides's *Guide of the Perplexed* close to the centre of the book. It is here (a section many readers skipped) that Benjamin found his passage, though he didn't really understand, or perhaps care to understand, its real meaning.

In a strikingly naturalistic moment of *The Guide*, Maimonides glosses the biblical statement that the two tablets of the Law which Moses brought down from Mount Sinai were "the work of God" to mean only that they were natural objects in a divinely created world. They were God's work merely in the sense in which He "planted" the cedars of Lebanon and all other trees. The two tablets of the Law were, argued Maimonides, entirely natural objects. The precise extent of Maimonides's naturalism here is controversial, but it was pushed to the limit by a daring fourteenth-century commentator named Moses of Narbonne, whom Maimon quoted in his autobiography:

> The stones of the mountain are engraved with the image
> of a bush and therefore it is called Mount Sinai, on
> account of the (burning) bush which God revealed to
> Moses there. And one of the notables of Barcelona, a son

of Ben Hasdai, brought me one of these stones and I saw the bush engraved upon it and this engraving is divine.
I broke the stone into pieces and the bush reappeared on every piece, and I broke these pieces and the bush reappeared on the surface of every fragment. I did this many times and still the bush reappeared. And I wondered at this and rejoiced greatly for it was a way to understand the meaning of our master Maimonides.

That is to say, the two stone tablets were the work of God in precisely the sense that every stone, tree, and other natural object is the work of God. They were inscribed, as the Bible has it elsewhere, "with the finger of God," in the sense that they were remarkably marked rocks. Moses of Narbonne, who in some respects anticipated Baruch Spinoza in his disenchanted naturalism, was making a point diametrically opposed to that of Walter Benjamin. Not only was the natural world not to be understood as divine language, the divinely inscribed tablets of Moses should be understood as merely natural. A description of the origin of Benjamin's stones is indeed in a medieval Hebrew text, but one he completely misunderstood. It was not a "Kabbalistic myth," it was an anti-mystical anecdote.

But what of the stones themselves? Although Benjamin had once remarked to Scholem that "a philosophy that does not include the possibility of soothsaying from coffee-grounds . . . cannot be a true philosophy," he seems to have thought of these stones of Sinai in entirely literary terms, never as rocks.

And yet, if Moses of Narbonne is to be believed, this is not a mythic text about divine language and the natural world; it is, in the first place, an anecdote about actual rocks, geological marvels. Were there such stones? And where would this Jewish notable of the Hasdai family have got them? The question becomes sharper when one realizes that the rabbinic tradition disavows and actively discourages any knowledge of the location of Sinai, perhaps because the mountain was associated with pre-Israelite worship. In any case, although Jews traveled to and from Jerusalem throughout the medieval period, and there were even claims by some Jewish travellers to have visited places with as much reality as Ultima Thule, no Jew ever claimed to have visited Sinai.

But medieval Christians did. There had been a monastery at the base of Jebel Musa, identified as Mount Sinai, since the fourth century. Later, in the ninth century, it became associated with Saint Catherine of Alexandria. So Moses of Narbonne's distinguished friend may have received the stones from a Christian pilgrim who had brought them back with him from Saint Catherine's Monastery. If this is the case, then it is perhaps the only instance of a Jewish-Christian trade in sacred relics, a shared sense that these stones carried with them an aura of holiness.

For there really were (and are) such stones at Mount Sinai, or at least at Jebel Musa. These "burning-bush stones" were prized by medieval Christian pilgrims, discussed and drawn by Early Modern Orientalists and biblical scholars, and even enjoyed a brief vogue in ultra-Orthodox Jewish circles in the 1970s and 1980s, though Rabbi Moses Feinstein, the leading authority of that world, was unimpressed. The presence of such stones at Sinai had been discussed as early as the thirteenth century by an Arab geographer named Ibn Yaqut, who, like Moses of Narbonne a century later, linked the geological phenomenon with the etymological tradition that "Sinai" meant tree or bush. Paul Maiberger, a German biblical scholar, published Ibn Yaqut's text in a little-read (but conventionally successful) *Habilitationsschrift* in 1984, and went on to speculate that it may have been precisely the presence of such stones that helped originally to make Sinai a holy site.

The rocks themselves are what geologists sometimes call pseudo-fossils, because they seem to clearly reproduce the image of a plant. In fact, the dendrite markings are the result of manganese crystallization in the cracks of the granite. When the granite is broken it naturally tends to break along these cracks, thus exposing further tree- or bush-like markings, though not ad infinitum, as Narboni claimed, and as Maimon (thinking, as it happens, of the theories of his acquaintance Goethe) and after him Benjamin, had been happy to accept.

Gershom Scholem believed that the subterranean tradition of Jewish mysticism might truly burst forth in the work of his friend Walter Benjamin, and he was constantly urging him to read in this tradition and make it his own. Their briefly shared plan for Benjamin to learn Hebrew had not been just another proposal for a paid holiday for a struggling intellectual; it had been an almost Messianic scheme to bring Benjamin into contact with the language of revelation. The first draft of Benjamin's prologue to *The Origin of German Tragic Drama*, with its talk of Adamic language, redemptive interpretation, and the miraculous stones of Sinai, was perhaps as close as Benjamin ever came to fulfilling Scholem's hopes for him. But the stones were not, as it turns out, the stuff of Kabbalistic myth; and Scholem (who might have told him so) probably never read that draft.

If Walter Benjamin had emigrated to Jerusalem in the 1930s (a lost possibility which Gershom Scholem spent the rest of his life mourning), he could, albeit with difficulty, even have visited Saint Catherine's Monastery and seen the stones of Sinai. Saint Catherine of Alexandria, who may never have existed, is, incidentally, the patron saint of philosophers and theologians.

Live Wire: Saul Bellow's
Life in Literature

IN *THE GHOST WRITER*, Philip Roth sends his fictional alter ego, a young Nathan Zuckerman, on a pilgrimage to discuss the life and art of fiction with the eminent writer E.I. Lonoff, a character clearly modeled on Bernard Malamud (with a bit of Henry Roth thrown in). Eventually they come to their greatest contemporary. "The disease of his life," Lonoff says, "makes Abravanel fly."

> I admire what he puts his nervous system through. I admire his passion for the front-row seat. Beautiful wives, beautiful mistresses, alimony the size of the national debt, polar expeditions, war-front reportage, famous friends, famous enemies, breakdowns, public lectures, five-hundred-page novels every third year, and still, as you said before, time and energy left over for all that self-absorption. The gigantic types in the books *have* to be that big to give him something to think about to rival himself. Like him? No. But, impressed, oh, yes. Absolutely. It's no pic-

nic up there in the egosphere. I don't know when the man sleeps, or if he has ever slept, aside from those few minutes when he had that drink with me.

Abravanel is even more clearly Saul Bellow (with, maybe, just a bit of Norman Mailer thrown in), who, according to Roth's recent chronicler Claudia Roth Pierpont, was not amused.

That Bellow's own fiction drew so heavily on his famously full and messy life has been both an obstacle and a blessing for his biographers. On the one hand, it is hard to wring new insight from situations and events that Bellow described and thought through so deeply, repeatedly, and vividly in his fiction. On the other, it is easier to correlate the life and the art when the novelist in question approaches fiction as "the higher autobiography."

Bellow's first would-be biographer was Mark Harris, a novelist and acquaintance who approached Bellow in the mid-1960s and self-consciously imagined himself playing Boswell to Bellow's Johnson. Bellow ducked and weaved for fifteen or so years until Harris—who is now remembered mostly for his baseball novel *Bang the Drum Slowly*—finally published *Saul Bellow, Drumlin Woodchuck*. It's an odd, charming memoir of his failures to pin down the elusive (and uncharmed) great author. The title is taken from Frost's famous poem in which the drumlin woodchuck's ". . . own strategic retreat/Is where two rocks almost meet,/ And still more secure and snug,/A two-door burrow I dug." A decade later, Ruth Miller, who had been among Bellow's first students in 1938 and a friend ever since, tried to corner him with a study called *Saul Bellow: A Biography of the Imagination*. It wasn't a great book; it was alternately chatty and ponderous, unsure whether it was a testimonial or a critical study, but it did hint at how much Bellow had drawn from his life for his fiction. They never spoke again.

Finally, in the 1990s, James Atlas was given full access to Bellow, his surviving family, friends, and papers (also his former friends, ex-wives, and enemies). Atlas succeeded in pinning Bellow down, and—to switch animals and famous poems (one Bellow once parodied in Yiddish, with his friend Isaac Rosenfeld)—when the novelist was pinned and wriggling on the wall, Atlas alternated between shrewd insight and a competitive, sneering condescension. (The refrain from Bellow and Rosenfeld's Prufrock parody reads *"Ikh ver alt, ikh ver alt/und der pupik vert mir kalt,"* roughly "I grow old, I grow old/and my belly button feels so cold.")

Three examples of Atlas' tone from early, middle, and late in the biography, taken almost at random: "Bellow's onerous duties as a parent didn't slow him down on the literary front," "it is a novel of ideas to put it in the kindest light," and, "After four marriages, Bellow was forced to acknowledge his shortcomings as a husband, but he continued to cast himself in the role of victim."

Bellow's new biographer Zachary Leader is authorized and judicious. His excellent biography, *The Life of Saul Bellow: To Fame and Fortune, 1915–1964*, was published on the occasion of what would have been Bellow's hundredth birthday—he made it to eighty-nine—as was a new collection of Bellow's essays, lectures and reviews, *There Is Simply Too Much to Think About*, edited by Benjamin Taylor. The two books nicely complement each other and both should push the reader back to the great fiction, which is in the end their justification.

Although Atlas did the initial spadework and interviewed many people who have since died, Leader has clearly done new and prodigious work in reconstructing and thinking through the details of a by-now familiar but still fascinating life, or rather the first half of it. Whereas Atlas took some 600 pages to tell almost the whole story (his *Bellow: A Biography* was published in 2000, five years before Bellow died), Leader takes almost 800 to get Bellow to the height of "fame and fortune," with the publication of *Herzog* in 1964, when Bellow was forty-nine. A second volume will carry Bellow through (to mention just some of the highlights) a Broadway flop, a bitter divorce and decade-long alimony battle, *Mr. Sammler's Planet*, co-editorship of several small literary magazines, journalism from Tel Aviv and Sinai in the midst of the Six-Day War, *Humboldt's Gift*, the Nobel Prize, marriage to a glamorous Rumanian mathematician, then another bitter divorce, and his brilliant late-life renaissance culminating in *Ravelstein*, his novel about—an imprecise but unavoidable preposition with Bellow—his friend and University of Chicago colleague Allan Bloom. And, of course, his final, and finally happy, marriage to Bloom's student Janis Freedman Bellow. It is hard not to be, like Roth's Lonoff, overwhelmed just thinking about the roiling turmoil and gigantic achievements of such a life.

SAUL BELLOW was born in 1915, in Lachine, Quebec, just outside of Montreal, but Leader begins with his father Abraham and the family's life in Russia. Abraham Belo (or Belous) was a volatile man, who had been briefly prosperous in Saint Petersburg before he was arrested for living there under false papers. The prosperity may have come from dealing in such papers (someone named "Belousov" was convicted of doing so around the same time, at any rate). Turn-of-the-century Russia is not Leader's scholarly beat, but he is rightly more interested in the Russia of family lore that eventually made it into Bellow's fiction than that of history. As Bellow once remarked "the retrospective was strong in me because of my parents," so Leader moves swiftly from the Russia of Abraham Belo's life to the old country that shadows his son's fiction. Soon we are hearing of Herzog's parents, who briefly lived, like

Bellow's, in a dacha in the old country, and of Pa Lurie in Bellow's unpublished manuscript from the 1950s, "Memoirs of a Bootlegger's Son," who was violent, "nervous like a fox," and escaped from "Pobedonosteyev's police" in Saint Petersburg, before eventually ending up in Chicago.

Bellow's mother died when he was in high school. It hit him hard, and his relationship with his father was never easy. Although Bellow was a tough guy in print, Bellow's father was a real tough guy, an operator who ended up running Chicago coal yards with his two older sons, and who could not understand his youngest or credit his success, even when it finally came. Of course, things were not quite that simple; his parents had read Tolstoy and the other great Russian novelists (Dostoevsky was to become Bellow's favorite). In an essay "On Jewish Storytelling," included in *There Is Simply Too Much to Think About*, Bellow credited him with his sense of narrative, or rather with his sense that everything was a story. "My father would say, whenever I asked him to explain any matter, 'The thing is like this: There was a man who lived . . .' [. . .] 'There once was a widow with a son . . .' 'A teamster was driving on a lonely road. . . .'" In *Seize the Day*, a beautiful novella published the year after Bellow's father had died, the protagonist Tommy Wilhelm is asked if he loves his aged, emotionally remote father:

> "Of course, of course I love him. My father. My mother—"
> As he said this there was a great pull at the very center
> of his soul. When a fish strikes the line you feel the live
> force in your hand. A mysterious being beneath the water,
> driven by hunger, has taken the hook and rushes away and
> fights, writhing.

Although it took him a while to find it—he was in his late thirties and had already written two novels—Bellow's first great subject was really his family and the Jewish Chicago in which he had grown up. He was in Paris on a Guggenheim fellowship, working on a depressing manuscript called "The Crab and the Butterfly," in which two invalids philosophize in a hospital ward. As he later told Philip Roth:

> I was walking heavyhearted toward my workplace one morning when I caught up with the cleaning crew who opened the taps at the street corners and let the water run along the curbs, flushing away the cigarette butts, dogs' caca, shredded letters, orange skins, candy wrappers into the large-mouthed sewers . . . Watching the flow, I felt less lame, and I was grateful for this hydrotherapy and the points of sunlight in it—nothing simpler.

Bellow walked away from the street washers repeating to himself "I am an American—Chicago born," at least so he remembered it in one version of the story (there were several and Leader quotes another variant). That is, he was suddenly writing the justly famous opening lines of *The Adventures of Augie March*:

> I am an American, Chicago born—Chicago, that somber city—and go at things as I have taught myself, free-style, and will make the record in my own way: first to knock, first admitted; sometimes an innocent knock, sometimes a not so innocent.

As Leader says, this is when Bellow "found his voice as a novelist," that distinctive freestyling prose that affects not to care exactly how its sprung rhythms and startling observations knock the reader. The last semi-grammatical phrase of that famous opening sentence, "sometimes a not so innocent," has an unabashed Yiddish flavor, while the one that follows reminds you that Augie is as American as Huck Finn but not unlettered:

> But a man's character is his fate, says Heraclitus, and
> in the end there isn't any way to disguise the nature of
> the knocks by acoustical work on the door or gloving
> the knuckles.

Bellow later spoke of his first two novels, *Dangling Man* and *The Victim*, as too proper, narrow, and constrained, an attempt, perhaps, to glove his knuckles or change the door.

Bellow's not so innocent knock is generally taken as the moment when Jews barged into American literature without apology, but it wasn't just a matter of voice. *Augie March* made an argument that the rough-and-tumble lives of Chicago Jews were as fit a subject for literature as any other. Standing there as the cleaning crew hosed down the Paris streets, Bellow says he thought of "a pal of mine whose surname was August—a handsome breezy freewheeling kid who used to yell out when we were playing checkers 'I got a scheme!'" Charlie August, like his later fictional counterpart, Augie March, was a social type of the 1920s and 1930s that basically no longer exists in America, a poor immigrant Jew:

> His father had deserted the family, his mother was, even
> to a nine-year-old kid, visibly abnormal, he had a strong
> and handsome older brother. There was a younger child
> who was retarded—a case of Down syndrome, perhaps—
> and they had a granny who ran the show. (She was not
> really the granny; she'd perhaps been placed there by a
> social agency that had some program for getting old peo-
> ple to take charge of broken families.)

This recollection, along with that of the street cleaners' "hydrotherapy," comes from the wonderful (if fragmentary and repetitive) written interview that Philip Roth conducted on and off with Bellow in the last years of his life and published in *The New Yorker* after his death. Leader draws upon it in his biography, and it is now the last main selection in Taylor's collection of Bellow's nonfiction.

Bellow said that Charlie August lived next door to him on West Augusta Boulevard, which is an Augustinian coincidence, though not impossible, even if it's an unlikely name for a Jew and the novel he ended up writing about him was cast as a kind of spiritual autobiography. He also said that he never knew what became of his pal, which is surprising, given that the book was a best-seller and the first chapters were a close, heartbreaking description of life in the March/August home. Wouldn't Charlie/Augie, or someone who knew him, have called? Everyone else Bellow ever wrote about seems to have. Atlas took this all at face value in his biography, but there is no indication that he checked it carefully, and I wonder if the Marches were a "purer," or at any rate more complicated, fictional invention than Bellow let on. Zachary Leader doesn't say this, but on the other hand he doesn't quite repeat Atlas' claim that the actual Augusts had the same familial set-up as the fictional Marches. Whatever the case here, one has the sense that, as a biographer, Leader has complete control of his material and does not feel the need to let the reader in on every calculation, contested reading, and judgment made in the back room.

Bellow gave Augie March many of his own adventures and experiences, from teenage jobs and pranks to his visit to Leon Trotsky in Mexico, only to find the great man dying in a hospital from the wounds of his pickaxe-wielding Stalinist assassin. And Augie's streetwise older brother Simon so closely resembles Bellow's older brother Maurice, down to the salacious details of a scandalous affair and love child, that it caused a rift between them. Years later,

Maurice's daughter Lynn said of her uncle "What kind of creative? He just wrote it down."

This was a frequent complaint from Bellow's friends, relatives, and acquaintances who did not realize that they were sitting for a portrait, or did realize but didn't like the way it came out. Not that he was easier on himself. *Herzog*, which is probably Bellow's best, most fully realized novel, is an account of an intellectual falling apart and pulling himself back together after discovering that his wife and best friend are lovers, which of course is what happened to Bellow.

As a truly literary biographer, Leader understands that what is important is how Bellow "wrote it down." In the case of the humble, mostly Jewish cast of characters in *The Adventures of Augie March*, one can see him asserting their significance as subjects from the very beginning, conjuring up the world of his childhood as he sits at a writing desk in Paris. Grandma Lausch, Augie's dictatorial matriarch who "wasn't really the granny," is described as "one of those Machiavellis of small street and neighborhood." Augie's description of his first great mentor, the devious crippled landlord-philosopher William Einhorn, sets out the theory behind this, what you might call Bellow's American aesthetic:

He had a brain and many enterprises, real directing power, philosophical capacity, and if I were methodical enough to take thought before an important and practical decision and also (N.B.) if I were really his disciple and not what I am, I'd ask myself "What would Caesar suffer in this case? What would Machiavelli advise or Ulysses do? What would Einhorn think?" I'm not kidding when I enter Einhorn in this eminent list. It was him that I knew, and what I understand of them in him. Unless you want to say that we're at the dwarf end of all times and mere children whose only share in grandeur is like a boy's share in fairy-tale kings, beings of a different kind from times better and stronger than ours.

Of Einhorn's wife, he writes, "While Mrs. Einhorn was a kind woman, ordinarily, now and again she gave me a glance that suggested Sarah and the son of Hagar."

There was no fairy tale time different and better and stronger than ours, or, even if there was, one is still obligated to live and reflect upon this age and one's own people. Of course, Mr. and Mrs. Einhorn were also based on figures in Bellow's life. They were the parents of his close friend, later enemy—he was his divorce attorney—Sam Freifeld, though it was a different friend, Dave Peltz, not Bellow or Charlie August, who really worked for them. As Leader quotes Bellow on the relation between fact and fiction: "The fact is a wire through which one sends a current. The voltage of that current is determined by the writer's own belief as to what matters, by his own caring or not-caring, by passionate choice."

It is perhaps this emphasis on literary art as the jolt of observant caring that brings memories and facts to life— as "when a fish strikes the line," and "you feel the live force in your hand"—that explains a puzzling feature of Bellow's work. He was, without a doubt, the most celebrated American novelist of his generation, winning every prize and most of them two or three times. But as compositions very few of the novels really hold together. Narrators over-share, narratives trail off, seemingly stray characters take over, and the individual elements of a novel can feel curiously unbalanced. The parts—breathtaking descriptions, brilliant dialogue, utterly original turns of phrase—often seem greater than the whole.

Philip Roth, Bellow's greatest champion, puzzled over this and once suggested that maybe he was in just too much of a hurry, which, in a way, is what Bellow himself wrote to Malamud in defense of *Augie March*: "A novel, like a letter, should be loose, cover much ground, run swiftly, take risk of mortality and decay." He wasn't aiming for a jeweler's perfection but rather to capture and requicken messy, creaturely, contingent moments of human life, when a "mysterious being beneath the water, driven by hunger, has taken the hook and rushes away and fights, writhing." And he loved a good joke.

Bellow's sense of the relation between life and literature and the purpose of the latter also helps to explain a curious feature of the non-fiction collected in *There Is Simply Too Much to Think About*. He was one of our great men of letters, the most discursive of fiction writers, a professor at the University of Chicago's Committee on Social Thought who seemingly gave lectures and wrote essays at the drop of an (elegant, rakish) hat, but he disdained literary critics and even the act of literary criticism. His own few reviews are more in the way of astringent encouragement of his peers. Reviewing Philip Roth's now-famous first book of short stories, *Goodbye, Columbus*, he wrote "Unlike those of us who came howling into the world, blind and bare, Mr. Roth appears with hair, nails and teeth, speaking coherently."

Critics ought to provide useful encouragement and then get the hell out of the way. This—as much as their differing temperaments and approaches—helps to explain the lifelong tension between Bellow and Lionel Trilling, the leading critic of his time, certainly among the Jewish intellectuals who came of age with Bellow in the 1930s. Invited to write a review of a new book of essays about Shakespeare's sonnets for Trilling's book club magazine *The Grif-*

fin, Bellow writes "Perhaps the pleasure this collection gives me is in part the pleasure of seeing modern critics working hard in the seventeenth century. It is like having mischievous children at last out of the house." Around this time, in the mid-1950s, Leader recounts a story of Bellow greeting Trilling at a party: "Still peddling the same old horseshit, Lionel?"

CALLING HIS Bellow-character "Abravanel" was a good joke, though one doubts that either Philip Roth or Bellow would have recognized Don Isaac Abravanel if he had stepped out of Ferdinand and Isabella's court and swatted them with a copy of his commentary to the *Guide of the Perplexed*. In the autobiographical lecture which opens *There Is Simply Too Much to Think About*, Bellow wrote that he had tried "to fit his soul into the Jewish-writer category but it does not feel comfortably accommodated there." And then comes the famous crack:

> I wonder now and then whether Philip Roth and Bernard Malamud and I have not become the Hart Schaffner and Marx of our trade. We have made it in the field of culture as Bernard Baruch made it on a park bench, as Polly Adler made it in prostitution, as Two-Gun Cohen, the personal bodyguard of SunYat-Sen, made it in China. My joke is not broad enough to cover the contempt I feel for the opportunists, wise guys and career types who impose such labels and trade upon them.

Roth and Malamud also resisted the category, but both of them made the meaning of Jewish identity a central problem in their fiction in ways that Bellow did not. Although Bellow was, intermittently, a spiritual seeker, his sense of Judaism, or rather Jewishness, was visceral, not intellectual. When William Faulkner advocated, as chairman of a distinguished committee of writers empanelled by President Eisenhower, freeing the fascist poet Ezra Pound, who had been tried for treason but found insane, Bellow wrote to him:

> Pound advocated in his poems and in his broadcasts enmity to the Jews and preached hatred and murder. Do you mean to ask me to join you in honoring a man who called for the destruction of my kinsmen? I can take no part in such a thing even if it makes for effective propaganda abroad, which I doubt. . . . Free him because he is a poet? Why, better poets than he were exterminated perhaps. Shall we say nothing in their behalf?

Bellow's unapologetic moral clarity here (and not only here) derived, in part, from the same intuition as the famous opening of *The Adventures of Augie March*: that one can be Jewish and entirely American. His job was to make something of that. As he wrote in an introduction to an anthology of Jewish stories: "We do not make up history and culture. We simply appear, not by our own choice. We make what we can of our condition with the means available. We must accept the mixture as we find it—the impurity of it, the tragedy of it, the hope of it." This was written in 1964, the last year Leader's first volume covers, but the sense of life and literature it expressed will carry his subject forward into the next volume. Bellow remained ineluctably Jewish and perpetually attuned to living in chaos.

This may be the key to understanding his life, his live-wire approach to artistic creation, even his jokes. A friend of mine was invited out to dinner with Bellow sometime in the 1990s. At the restaurant, his wife urged him to order healthily, to which Bellow replied "enough of this *Tofu va-vohu*!"—*Tohu va-vohu* being, of course, the book of Genesis' description for the chaos out of which God created the universe.

Shades of Frost: A Hidden Source for Nabokov's *Pale Fire*

VLADIMIR NABOKOV'S first, fumbling biographer, Andrew Field, almost found it, when he asked the author about the connection between John Shade, the fictional poet of *Pale Fire*, and Robert Frost. Nabokov teasingly replied, as he had before, that he really knew only one short poem by Frost. Although puzzled, Field didn't press the matter and apparently never asked precisely which poem of Frost's it was that Nabokov knew.

But Field was right to wonder. Nabokov gave two poetry readings with Robert Frost, in 1942 and 1945, and was, along with Frost, Archibald Macleish, and T. S. Eliot, one of four speakers who appeared in Wellesley College's "Poets Reading" series in 1946. He also met Frost at least once socially, though he found him rude. Their second joint poetry reading was at Filene's Department Store in Boston to an audience assembled to hear New England's leading poet, not Nabokov. Nabokov read his recently composed "An Evening of Russian Poetry," which is about the virtual impossibility of writing poetry in English as a Russian exile. Not coincidentally, this is closely related to the difficulty of serving as the warm-up act for Robert Frost before an American audience. The poem is a dazzling success:

> Beyond the seas where I have lost a scepter,
> I hear the neighing of my dappled nouns,
> Soft participles coming down the steps,
> Treading on leaves and trailing their rustling gowns. . . .

Seven years later, in 1952, Nabokov and his wife even briefly rented Frost's house in Cambridge, Massachusetts. They found it too cold to stay in, but amusing to later pun about ("the Jack Frost house"). It also troubled Nabokov that Frost had left the study at the center of the house locked. Through his early years in America, Nabokov seemed to shadow Frost. So Field had grounds for suspecting that the relationship between John Shade and Robert Frost was more than superficial, but he did not pursue these suspicions.

Pale Fire is Nabokov's most allusive puzzle novel. Its relation to its sources is central both to its interpretation and the reader's enjoyment. As Mary McCarthy wrote in the opening lines of her famous early review, it is:

> A Jack-in-the-Box . . . a chess problem, an infernal machine. . . . When the separate parts are assembled, according to the manufacturer's directions, and fitted together with the help of clues and cross-references, which must be hunted down as in a paper-chase, a novel on several levels is revealed.

McCarthy herself chased down several allusions and solved some intricate problems. Over the past five decades a fantastically ingenious body of *Pale Fire* scholarship has developed. But the seemingly simple question of the relationship between the fictional Shade and the actual Frost has been touched on only glancingly, and unsatisfactorily.

The four parts of Nabokov's infernal fiction machine are, in order: a foreword by the homosexual expatriate scholar Charles Kinbote, who thinks he is the exiled King of Zembla; an all-but-finished 999-line poem called "Pale Fire," in four cantos, by Kinbote's neighbor, the great American poet John Shade; Kinbote's comically self absorbed commentary; and, finally, a similarly idiosyncratic index, salted with hidden clues. Each of these parts supplements and corrects, reflects and distorts, the others, bringing out one character, thematic intricacy, or narrative detail, while hiding another.

Midway through the poem, the fictional relation between Shade and Robert Frost is made explicit. While waiting for their awkward daughter, who will never, in this life, return from her first, disastrous date, Shade and his wife catch a bit of literary chatter on television:

I was in time to hear brief fame
And have a cup of tea with you: my name
Was mentioned twice, as usual just behind
(One oozy footstep) Frost.

The critical consensus in our own literary world has, if anything, been less generous. Michael Wood writes in *The Magician's Doubts*: "Shade resembles Frost a little: in looks; slow, sly style of wit; fund of wily common sense. He is a milder character than Frost though; kinder; and a lot more than a footstep behind him as a poet." One could add that both Shade and Frost are regional poets with cool, climatic names, taught at distinguished universities, wrote poems with birds and butterflies, lost a child to suicide, bore a distinguished owlish look in old age, and so on. But, given all of this, not to speak of Nabokov's many unsatisfactory meetings and non-meetings with the poet, might there also be a closer literary connection between Robert Frost and Nabokov's (or is it Frost's?) Shade?

Wood does make a more substantive comparison between Frost and Shade a little later. In the fourth canto, John Shade detects (desperately, poignantly, but also trenchantly) signs of artistic design in the arrangements of his universe. His "feeling of fantastically planned,/richly rhymed life," together with certain coincidences, premonitions and ethereal hints give him an intimation of an afterlife which his daughter might inhabit. Shade goes on:

> I feel I understand
> Existence, or at least a minute part
> Of my existence, only through my art,
> In terms of combinational delight;
> And if my private universe scans right,
> So does the verse of galaxies divine
> Which I suspect is an iambic line.
> I'm reasonably sure that we survive
> And that my darling somewhere is alive. . . .

Wood finds this aesthetic theodicy, which Nabokov certainly shared with Shade, profoundly unappealing, and compares it to Frost's famous sonnet of a spider and its prey:

> Shade is several footsteps behind Robert Frost here, who knew that even Nature's intricate arrangements, let alone ours, can "appall" us; that a pattern of whitenesses, spider, flower, moth, may add up to a "design of darkness."

Frost's "Design" ("What brought the kindred spider to that height/Then steered the white moth thither in the night?") is also about the seeming artistry of nature and the problem of evil, though it comes to a conclusion that admits no shade of Nabokovian consolation. ("Read the poem 'Design,' and see if you sleep the better for it," Lionel Trilling told a shocked crowd gathered to celebrate Frost's birthday, in 1959.) But Wood's comparison is unduly harsh, almost as unfair as his re-use of that "more than a footstep" quip. Nature, in all its intricate "plexed artistry," can bear opposing interpretations, if anything can, and theodicy can be a deep recognition of the terrors of life as well as a retreat from them. Frost was a greater American poet than Nabokov (who could deny it?), but it wasn't because he was a homespun stoic and Nabokov a dandyish Neo-Platonist. In any event, the comparison brings us no closer to a source for *Pale Fire* in the poetry of Frost.

In his commentary, Kinbote adduces Frost's "Stopping by Woods on a Snowy Evening" when the comparison between Shade and Frost comes up, and describes it as "a poem that every American boy knows by heart." But every reader of *Pale Fire* knows not to trust mad Kinbote, who thinks that "Pale Fire" is a poem about his exile from the kingdom of Zembla (he imagines that he has really lost a scepter, and longs for ephebic royal pages, not dappled nouns), and not about (among other things) a father's grief at his daughter's suicide. Kinbote even famously misses the Shakespearean allusion that gives the work its "moondrop title." The relevant lines from *Timon of Athens* (which Kinbote just happens to quote elsewhere, from a comically mangled Zemblan translation) are:

> The sun's a thief and with his great attraction
> Robs the vast sea; the moon's an arrant thief,
> And her pale fire she snatches from the sun. . . .

What, if any, pale fire did Nabokov snatch from Frost? The imagery, meter, and mood of "Stopping by Woods on a Snowy Evening" are glaringly absent from Shade's poem (though they are both wintry lyrics). Is there another "short poem" concealed behind Kinbote's misdirection? If there is, it might also reveal something of the improvised methods and secret stratagems by which Nabokov managed to enter, appropriate, and even command the poetic tradition to which Frost was heir, in which his Russian scepter was powerless, his dappled nouns a distant memory.

In a much discussed 2004 article in the *Times Literary Supplement*, Michael Maar announced his discovery that there was an earlier fictional nymphet named Lolita, who had appeared in a 1916 German short story by Heinz von Lichberg, and argued that Nabokov had probably read but subsequently forgotten the story during his years in Berlin. Thus, his later coupling of name and theme was a case of "cryptomnesia." With regard to *Pale Fire* and a particular short poem by Frost—which is not "Stopping by Woods on a Snowy Evening"—I claim neither "cryptomnesia" nor, certainly, plagiarism, but rather a delicate but demonstrable network of inspiration and allusion. This discovery is both less surprising (every reader of *Pale Fire* knows that John Shade resembles Robert Frost) and more revealing, for it shows Nabokov in the act of conscious composition and similarly conscious camouflage.

"I am," Nabokov liked to say (especially after moving to Switzerland), "as American as apple pie." "Pale Fire," the poem, was his best evidence for the claim. Of all his narrators, only John Shade has the memories, cadences, and (more or less) the vocabulary of an American. In *Pale Fire*, puzzles about doubles, ghostly shades, and shadowy figures (who is reflecting whom?) abound. Here, as elsewhere, Nabokov's narrative play is underwritten by a deep interest in the existence of other worlds and their relationship to one another: that of the author and his artistic creation; of homeland and exile; of fictions within fictions and of mortal life and its possible successor. Each of these paired worlds, and others, are present in the justly famous and thematically crucial opening couplets of "Pale Fire":

> I was the shadow of the waxwing slain
> By the false azure in the windowpane;
> I was the smudge of ashen fluff—and I
> Lived on, flew on, in the reflected sky.

We shall return to these lines, but it's worth noting that they also initiate the pervasive avian imagery of *Pale Fire*. More than a dozen species of bird fly through its pages; Shade describes his favorite seat on the porch as "a nest," and his parents were ornithologists. This makes the book unique in the Nabokov corpus, where butterflies (which play a crucial, if less visible, role here as well) famously predominate. In 1962, in an interview shortly after the publication of *Pale Fire*, Nabokov slyly underscored the importance of birds to his novel while pointedly avoiding discussing its origins:

> All I know is that at a very early stage of the novel's development, I get this urge to gather bits of straw and fluff, and to eat pebbles. Nobody will ever discover how clearly a bird visualizes, or if it visualizes at all, the future nest and the eggs in it.

In fact, Nabokov had been blocked in the composition of *Pale Fire*, and collecting bits of literary debris, from 1957 to 1960. A letter to his editor Jason Epstein in March, 1957, describes a work in which, as Brian Boyd notes in his indispensable biography, "there is still no Shade, no homosexual king, no poem, commentary, and index." A few months later, in October, Nabokov jotted down the following note on an index card: "Waxwings: knocking themselves out in full flight against the reflected world of our picture window. Leaving a little gray fluff on the pane." Not until much later does he seem to realize that the observation might be a part of his novel-in-progress.

The hints that some particular poem of Frost's was crucially important for *Pale Fire* actually begin in the second paragraph of Kinbote's Foreword, where he meticulously describes Shade's manuscript. "The short Canto One," he writes, "with all those amusing birds and parhelia, occupies thirteen cards." The reader may be excused for gliding over the obscure second term, especially since he has not, at this point, read the canto being described. The reader who knows that a parhelion is a mock-sun—a kind of pale fire—may connect it with any one of the many poetic allusions in the first canto (to Wordsworth's "Prelude," say, or to Pope). But the meteorological phenomenon in question is produced by the refraction of the sun's rays through the prism of an ice crystal. In short, it is a form of pale fire produced when the sun's light shines through a kind of atmospheric frost.

IN 2004, on NABOKV-L (an unusually productive web-based discussion forum), Kenneth Tapscott suggested Frost's "New Hampshire" as a possible source for "Pale Fire." This has some merit. Frost's 1923 poem mocks an institution dedicated to conversations with the dead, as does Shade's. Frost's is called "The S'ciety for Psychical Research," and Shade's is the "Institute (I) of Preparation (P)/For the Hereafter (H), or IF. . . ." The former might have suggested the latter, but, unfortunately, nothing in the date, form, or content of the poems tends to corroborate it. "New Hampshire" is one of Frost's first self-indulgent blank-verse rambles. Moreover, it is, at almost 500 lines, not the single short Frost poem Nabokov admitted to knowing.

It is time to return to Kinbote, as unreliable as he is. In his commentary to the "oozy footstep" line, he writes:

> The line displays one of those combinations of pun and metaphor at which our poet excels. In the temperature charts of poetry high is low, and low high, so that the degree at which perfect crystallization occurs is above that of tepid facility.

Despite the madness, Kinbote is a perceptive reader of poetry, and he is right to call our attention to the importance of temperature in these lines. Shade's self-deprecating play on Frost's name suggests, fairly or not, that his lines may be slushy in places where they aspire to the harder clarity of a frost crystal. Indeed, the standard of beauty throughout *Pale Fire* is that of literally crystalline symmetry, and the idea and image of an ice crystal recur throughout. When a snowflake settles on Shade's watch, he remarks "crystal to crystal." At the outset of the poem, Shade describes the winter view outside his window as a "crystal land," to which Kinbote remarks "Perhaps a reference to Zembla, my dear country," superimposing his delusional world on Shade's artistic one. Perhaps most tellingly, Kinbote argues that the missing 1000th line of the poem must be a repetition of its opening line, "I was a shadow of the waxwing slain," by saying, "I cannot imagine that he [Shade] intended to deform the faces of his crystal." (Thomas Bolt picks up on this ice-crystal aesthetic in his 1001-line homage to *Pale Fire*, "Dark Ice.")

The balance of Kinbote's commentary on the "oozy footstep line" is comically fatuous, but indirectly revealing.

> Robert Frost (b. 1874) . . . Frost is the author of one of the greatest short poems in the English language, a poem that every American boy knows by heart, about

wintry woods, and the dreary dusk, and the little horsebells of gentle remonstration in the dull darkening air,
and that prodigious and poignant end—two closing
lines identical in every syllable, but one personal and
physical, and the other metaphysical and universal. I
dare not quote from memory lest I displace one small
precious word.

 With all his excellent gifts, John Shade could never
make *his* snowflakes settle that way.

This is almost true—Kinbote's admirable scruples notwithstanding, he manages to replace Frost's descriptive
"harnessbells" with meaningless "horsebells"—and almost
fair. However, the judgment that "Shade could never make
his snowflakes settle that way" is of little help in understanding the poetry before us (poems, like snowflakes,
being unique). Suppose we take this as a clue, and focus
on Shade's poetic snowfall rather than Frost's. The second
stanza, which follows the slain waxwing, begins: "Retake
the falling snow: each drifting flake/Shapeless and slow,
unsteady and opaque." A few lines later, I read Nabokov as
slyly underlining the question of the relation of Frost's brilliant verse to that of his apparent shade:

And in the morning, diamonds of frost
Express amazement: Whose spurred feet have crossed
From left to right the blank page of the road?
Reading from left to right in winter's code:
A dot, an arrow pointing back; repeat:
Dot, arrow pointing back . . . A pheasant's feet!
Torquated beauty, sublimated grouse,
Finding your China right behind my house.
Was he in *Sherlock Holmes*, the fellow whose
Tracks pointed back when he reversed his shoes?

Kinbote's commentary leaves "the diamonds of frost" on "the blank page of the road" unremarked, but tells us, helpfully, that Sherlock Holmes was:

A hawk-nosed, lanky, rather likable private detective, the main character in various stories by Conan Doyle. I have no means to ascertain at the present time which of these is referred to here but suspect that our poet simply made up the Case of the Reversed Footprints.

As many have noted, Shade didn't invent the backward-shoes image. It was Holmes himself who suggested the ruse as one way he might have left the impression that he had fallen over Reichenbach Falls together with Professor Moriarty. More to our point, the lines suggest both that there may be a mystery and that Kinbote is an Anglo-American illiterate. His comment on Sherlock Holmes is of a piece with his remarks on "On Stopping by Woods on a Snowy Evening." They both leave literary tracks pointing in the wrong direction.

Before turning to the right one, I want to examine one more (almost) blind alley. In addition to supposed variants, Kinbote quotes several other poems of Shade's. None of these is clearly modeled on a poem by Frost, but the publication details of perhaps the most important of them is given. "The Nature of Electricity" was, Kinbote tells us, "sent to the New York magazine *The Beau and the Butterfly*, sometime in 1958." It is a curious fact of American literary history that Robert Frost never published in the *New Yorker* (whose famous first cover featured a dandy peering at a butterfly through his monocle) in 1958 or in any other year. Nonetheless, it is a likely time for a Frost poem to have caught Nabokov's eye. As we have seen, he was trying to write what would become *Pale Fire*, collecting "bits of straw and fluff and eating pebbles," and yet had not struck on almost any of the elements which would later comprise the novel. In particular, he did not have a poet (American or otherwise), a commentary, or an avian theme.

The cover of *The Saturday Review of Literature* for April 12, 1958, featured a close-up of the by-now iconic Frost, looking much as Nabokov would later describe John Shade, staring out from under "a hoary forelock," with "all his wrinkles beaming." At the time, the *Saturday Review* was still just a step behind the *New Yorker* in icy wit, literary reputation, and sophisticated readership. Nabokov regularly read it along with the *New Yorker* and the *Atlantic* and continued to do so even after he moved to Montreux in Switzerland. Inside this particular issue was a commentary by John Ciardi (an acquaintance of Nabokov's) on Frost's "Stopping By Woods on a Snowy Evening," which was reproduced at the beginning of the piece. The essay is characteristically shrewd, and Kinbote's remarks on the poem seem to have profited from it. Ciardi also remarked on a characteristic of Frost's compositional habits, which Nabokov shared and made sure to give to Shade: "Robert Frost is the sort of artist who hides his traces. I know of no Frost worksheets anywhere. . . . Frost would not willingly allow anything but the finished product to leave him." Finally, in the back of the magazine was a new short poem by Frost, about a bird and a sky-reflecting window:

> The Winter owl banked just in time to pass
> And save herself from breaking window glass.
> And her wide wings strained suddenly aspread
> Caught color from the last of evening red
> In a display of underdown and quill
> To glassed-in children at the windowsill.

This, I submit, is the "one short poem of Frost's" that Nabokov truly "knew," in the intimate sense of having appropriated it for his art. Frost's poem, "Of a Winter Evening" (only a step away from the much more famous title), depicts the near collision of a bird with a sky-reflecting window, features a neat reversal of perspective, and is in heroic couplets. Both Kinbote and Michael Wood emphasized the metaphysical lightness of Shade's verse in comparison to Frost, but here something like the opposite seems to be the case. Frost's poem dramatizes the confrontation between humans and nature in miniature, and is performed with characteristic dexterity. It is a minor poem from a major poet. The first stanza of "Pale Fire" takes a similar scenario and poetic form in a much more elaborately discursive, metaphysical direction. Frost's striking description of "glassed-in children" also seems to have acted on Nabokov's imagination. Figures are repeatedly glassed-in in *Pale Fire*, from the narrator who identifies with the waxwing from behind the fatal pane to Kinbote discussing the posthumous publication of Shade's poem with a publisher while encased "in a cell of walnut and glass." Shade's Aunt Maud spent her last days in a sanitarium sitting in Pinedale's "glassed sun." After her death, we learn that she left among her effects a paperweight "of convex glass, enclosing a lagoon." Each of these images is what Robert Alter has called an "ideogram of the novel," which exhibits in miniature what Shade senses about his world, that we are "most artistically caged" by some higher authorial being.

IN THE SPRING of 1958, Nabokov was still in the midst of his seemingly endless commentary on Pushkin's great verse novel *Eugene Onegin*, which also included a foreword and an index. He had already observed misguided waxwings crashing against his window, and even composed a narrative in heroic couplets, "The Ballad of Longwood Glen," which he had recently revised and published in the *New Yorker*, though it was a much lighter poem than his eventual "Pale Fire." He was also contemplating a novel which involved an exiled king (though he was neither a homosexual nor a literary commentator) and the question of immortality. When Nabokov read "Of a Winter Evening," after almost two decades of American exile in which he seemed to be always shadowing Frost, it combined with these and other elements in his kaleidescopic imagination. As Charles Kinbote says of Shade:

> I am witnessing a unique physiological phenomenon: John Shade perceiving and transforming the world, taking it in and taking it apart, re-combining its elements in the very process of storing them up so as to produce at some unspecified date an organic miracle, a fusion of image music, a line of verse.

What Kinbote omits is precisely the question of literary influence—that the world is always transformed in the light of earlier transformations—but, then, even the moon's a thief. On November 29, 1960, in Nice (the date is preserved in his manuscript), Nabokov began his poetic parhelion about a bird:

> I was the shadow of the waxwing slain
> By the false azure in the windowpane

Nabokov was, like Frost and Shade, the sort of artist who hid his traces, and the manuscript of *Pale Fire* now in the Library of Congress is a clean fair copy with few signs of "the fluff and pebbles" with which he began. Nonetheless, it is worth noting that both Shade's Sherlock Holmes couplet (which was, at first, uncharacteristically clumsy: "Fellow in Sherlock Holmes tried to confuse/Pursuit by putting on backwards his shoes") and Kinbote's comment on Frost, Shade and the "temperature charts of poetry," are thoroughly reworked. It was clearly important to Nabokov to leave a telltale hint of Holmesian mystery in those footprints on the "diamonds of frost," even before the perfect couplet came to him, and later to handle the Frost-frost-Shade connection in Kinbote's comment with precision.

1962, when *Pale Fire* was published, was also the year that Frost published *In the Clearing*, his final book. "Of a Winter Evening" was included, but Frost re-titled it "Questioning Faces." In doing so, he had unknowingly helped to erase the paper trail to the poem whose reflected light shines from the opening lines of "Pale Fire," and without which Nabokov's novel is almost unimaginable.

Cynthia Ozick's *Dictation*

IN A REVIEW of Saul Bellow's *Him With His Foot in His Mouth*, a book of five short stories, Cynthia Ozick asked:

> Does there come a time when, out of the blue, an author offers to decode himself? Not simply to divert, or paraphrase, or lead around a corner, or leave clues, or set out decoys (familiar apparatus, art-as-usual), but . . . spill wine all over the figure in the carpet . . . and disclose the thing itself? To let loose, in fact, the secret? . . . The cumulative art, concentrated, so to speak, in a vial?

Now, at a similarly late stage in her career, Ozick has collected four stories of her own, "a quartet," as the subtitle of her new book has it, and one is tempted to ask the same question. Has Ozick offered to decode herself?

Perhaps—though it should be noted that it was never clear that Bellow's one true subject, his "secret," was, as Ozick claimed, "the Eye of God" ("the Wit of Saul" might come closer). Ozick is, like Bellow, known as a Jewish writer, but unlike Bellow, who once criticized Isaac Bashevis Singer as "too Jewy," she has not resisted the label or dismissed it as socio-historical happenstance. To the contrary,

133

the question of what it means to write as a Jew has always been at the center of Ozick's work.

Her first published short story, "The Pagan Rabbi" (1966), depicts a rabbinic scholar who tells his children fantastic tales, comes to worship nature, and, in a fit of despair and ecstasy, ends up hanging himself from a tree with his *tallit* (prayer shawl). The central character of her most successful novel, *The Cannibal Galaxy* (1983), is a Jewish educator whose great ambition is to lead a school that marries the best of the Jewish and classical traditions; he fails. Ozick's 2004 novel *Heir to the Glimmering World* manages to be at once about a figure very much like Christopher Milne, the unhappy model for his father's "Winnie the Pooh" stories, and about the medieval Jewish heresy of Karaism, which rejected rabbinic commentary in favor of biblical literalism.

Ozick, of all Jewish American writers, has been most concerned with God and His demands. Not the "God-idea," or ecstatic spiritual experience, but the biblical God of Sinai Who announces Himself as utterly unique and prohibits the worship of anything else or its image "in the form of the heaven above, or on the earth beneath, or in the water under the earth."

Is art, then—the image-making and image-worshiping activity par excellence—a violation of God's command? Is art idolatrous? This conundrum underlies Ozick's fiction and has inspired some of her most incisive criticism. Her answer would appear to be a tough-minded yes, with the caveat that the conundrum is also inescapable. Art for art's sake *is*, in Ozick's judgment, the worship of images, lumps of inert clay or heaps of mere words. But writers and artists necessarily come to the beauty of the created world late, and in their rapture cannot help wishing to usurp the primal creativity, rivaling God and proclaiming their human handiwork very good. For a Jewish author, one who aims to be not just ethnically but theologically Jewish, the only recourse—and it is but partial—is to make her art moral.

Critics have sometimes treated the relationship of Ozick's iconoclastic criticism to her own fiction as theory to practice, charging her with inconsistency. As if, Ozick once tartly noted, the essays provided "chalk marks . . . to take the measure of the stories." A better approach is to read both Ozick's fiction and her essays as composed out of the selfsame tension between the monotheistic ban on idolatry and the desire to usurp God by creating beauty. In *Dictation*, this theme is distilled, "concentrated, so to speak, in a vial," despite the fact that its best stories are not ostensibly about Jews or Judaism.

At forty-seven small pages, the title story "Dictation," is not really, as the publisher's jacket copy has it, "a novella." It has more of the static, schematic subtlety of an allegory. Set in England at the turn of the twentieth century, it tells (or rather makes up) the story behind the very proper, slightly tense relationship between the novelists Henry James and Joseph Conrad. James is, for Ozick, the unexcelled genius of the art of fiction. But this compliment, as we have seen, is bound to be ambivalent. Indeed, she has told the story of her own artistic maturation as an escape from James's influence, and described her first novel *Trust* (1966) as a Jamesian failure.

In the opening scene of "Dictation," a nervous, unproven Conrad—he has not yet published *Heart of Darkness*—visits James, already "the Master," in his London flat. There, Conrad sees a startlingly impersonal new instrument, the Remington typewriter with which James writes:

On a broad surface reserved for it in a far corner . . . stood the Machine . . . headless and armless and legless—brute shoulders merely: it might as well have been the torso of a broken god.

Later, thinking about James, Conrad muses that "the Master's cosmopolitanism, his civilized restraint, his perfection of method, his figures so finished, chiseled, and carved, were, when you came down to it, stone."

If a pagan sees gods everywhere, Ozick sees idols. James's "figures," his characters, are potential idols precisely because they are too perfect: the flesh of character so finely delineated that it becomes bloodless stone. The typewriter is likewise an idol because it intervenes between the creator and the created, mystifying the creative process.

James had hired an amanuensis or typist "who recorded in shorthand James's dictation and then transcribed it on the Machine; but it soon turned out to be more efficient to speak directly to the thing itself, with [the typist] at the keys." A decade later, Conrad would have his own typewriter and typist, a fragile, besotted young woman named Lillian Hallowes, and the two writers, unbeknownst to each other, would both be working on *doppelgänger* tales: Conrad on "The Secret Sharer" and James on "The Jolly Corner," about a man who confronts the ghost of the person he might have been. Inevitably, though each of their employers intuitively disapproves, Hallowes meets her opposite number, James's amanuensis Theodora Bosanquet, an altogether more forceful character.

In "Dictation," Ozick has created an elegant hall of mirrors: two authors, two typists, two stories, each about a protagonist and his double, and, finally, two passages of prose, one by Conrad that is almost Jamesian and another by James that sounds almost like Conrad. Out of this delirious twinning Miss Bosanquet, who is described at one point as an "idolatrous healer," contrives her own elegant plot for immortality, something halfway between a literary prank (another bit of secret sharing) and a diabolical usurpation.

This is a brilliant variation on Ozick's fundamental theme of art as idolatry. But does it work as a story? Here and elsewhere, Ozick dazzles more than she engages. Neither Conrad nor James really comes alive, their own figures seeming not so much chiseled stone as characters in a PBS costume drama. The allegory can be decoded—Bosanquet the usurper is to James as James is to God, and so on—but the plot fails, finally, to satisfy.

The theme of art as usurpation, or secret sharing, is also at the center of "Actors," the second story in the collection, featuring a mediocre television actor named Matt Sorley ("born Mose Sadacca") who attempts to re-create the histrionic grandeur of a Yiddish actor of the old school only to be vanquished by a kind of ghost. But the real twin of "Dictation," and the other immensely ambitious story of this collection, is "At Fumicaro."

The story's protagonist, Frank Castle, is a middle-aged Catholic journalist who attends a conference in Mussolini's Italy, before America has entered the war, on "The Church and How It Is Known." The conference is just as boring as it sounds, and yet it, or rather Castle's failure to attend very much of it, changes his life. Upon arriving in his room, he finds the teen-aged chambermaid retching over his toilet. "In four days," Ozick writes, "she would be his wife."

Castle sees her at first not as a suffering human being or even as an object of desire but as a beautiful object:

> The woman went on vomiting. . . . Watching serenely, he thought of some grand fountain where dolphins, or else infant cherubim, spew foamy white water from their bottomless throats. He saw her shamelessly: she was a solid little nymph. She was the coarse muse of Italia. He recited to himself, *If to any man the tumult of the flesh were silenced, silenced the phantasies of earth, water, and air, silenced, too, the poles.*

The passage in italics is, oddly, St. Augustine's attempt to describe the abstract beauties of heaven to his dying mother, and yet within two hours Castle has seduced this teenager, who is in fact already pregnant (hence the nausea).

Castle's first image of his future wife is as carved stone. But, to his chagrin, it is she who is "in thrall to sticks and stones"—ready to pray, it seems, almost anywhere and to almost anything: a decayed bit of Roman statuary on the roadside, which she insists on addressing as Saint Francis, kitschy icons of Jesus and the Madonna whose vividness is "*molto sacro*," museum pieces, and, in the final scene, the endless "saints and martyrs and angels and gryphons and gargoyles and Romans" at the top of the Milan cathedral. It is here that Castle has an epiphany concerning the consequences of idolatry that he finds both hilarious and humiliating. "'You could be up here,' he said—now he understood exactly what had happened at Fumicaro; he had fixed his penance for life—'a thousand years!'"

Ozick's oeuvre is not exhausted by the question of idolatry. Even in this collection, the story that rounds out the quartet, "But What Happened to the Baby?" does not really fit the pattern. It is also, as it happens, the least successful of the four stories: a dark joke about Esperanto in the Catskills with an O. Henry twist that doesn't quite carry narrative conviction.

Nonetheless, if any writer has a grand metaphor, a secret, the thing itself at the center of the maze, it is Ozick. That ineffable thing is God, or, more precisely if also more negatively, the fact that nothing in this world, no matter how beautiful, *is* a god.

Modern Jewish thought may be said to have begun with Moses Mendelssohn's argument at the end of the eighteenth century that Judaism remained valid and still necessary in the world of the Enlightenment as the religion that rejected all idolatries. With a little license, one could say that modern Jewish literature began at the outset of the twentieth century with Saul Tchernikovsky's Hebrew poem, "Before the Statue of Apollo," which laments that very same rejection. Even when she is not entirely successful, Cynthia Ozick is, alone among the major Jewish American writers, a conscious heir to both traditions.

It's Spring Again:
Don DeLillo on Resurrection

As EVERYONE KNOWS, April is the cruelest month, though even English majors sometimes forget why the poet said so. What's wrong with lilacs coming out of the dead land? Something to do with a then-repressed Christianity and a bad marriage (or vice versa), a disinclination to have the spring rain stir dull roots, or anything else. Although I am inclined to think that after the Holocaust Eliot mostly repented of his anti-Semitism, I still prefer Cole Porter ("I love you/Hums an April breeze").

Of course, the specifically Christian backdrop of Eliot's lines is the New Testament account of Jesus' resurrection in springtime. Curiously, when, fifty or so lines later, Eliot gets to the famous tarot card stanza, "the hanged man" card is supposed to represent Jesus, along with Frazer's pagan man-god, who must be slain and replaced so that the world can be renewed. I suppose that it is just a coincidence that the rabbis' old polemical description of Jesus was "the hanged one."

The backdrop, in turn, of the Christian belief in resurrection is not merely, or mainly, pagan. It is a central, and unsettling, dogma of rabbinic Judaism that, as the second blessing of the *Shemoneh Esreh* states, God "sustains the living with kindness and revives the dead with great mercy." At the end of this blessing, there is even a whiff of spring: "Who is like you, lord of power, and who is similar to you, O King, who brings death and revives life, and causes salvation to sprout," which sounds a little like the return of those lilacs that Eliot dreaded.

The connection between springtime and the messianic resurrection of the dead is even clearer in the *haftarah* for the Sabbath that falls in the middle of Passover. The prophetic reading the rabbis chose is Ezekiel's vision of the revival of the dry bones:

> I prophesied as I had been commanded. And while I was
> prophesying, suddenly there was a sound of rattling, and
> the bones came together, bone to matching bone. I looked,
> and there were sinews on them, and flesh had grown,
> and skin had formed over them; but there was no breath
> in them. Then He said to me, "Prophesy to the breath,
> prophesy, O mortal! Say to the breath: Thus said the Lord
> God: Come, O breath, from the four winds, and breathe
> into these slain, that they may live again." I prophesied as
> He commanded me. The breath entered them, and they
> came to life and stood up on their feet, a vast multitude
> (Ezekiel 37: 7–10).

A startling painting on the walls of the ancient synagogue at Dura Europos depicts this scene. There one finds some second-century Jews who have, until recently, been dead and who look very surprised to have been reconstituted and revived. Alongside them are various body parts—heads, arms, legs—that have yet to be re-membered, as it were. (ISIS has apparently looted the original archaeological site of Dura Europos near the Euphrates, but the paintings remain, at least for now, in the National Museum of Damascus.)

Of course, the plain meaning of Ezekiel's vision is that it is an allegory, indeed one that God himself interprets:

> And He said to me, "O mortal, these bones are the whole House of Israel. They say, 'Our bones are dried up, our hope is gone; we are doomed.' Prophesy, therefore, and say to them: Thus said the LORD God: I am going to open your graves and lift you out of the graves, O My people, and bring you to the land of Israel" (Ezekiel 37: 11–13).

This prophecy of national renewal is the reason the rabbis chose Chapter 37 of Ezekiel to read on Passover. And yet, as Jon D. Levenson showed in his *Resurrection and the Restoration of Israel*, the promise of Israel's revival was not held entirely distinct from the promise of an actual revival of the dead at the end of times.

By the early rabbinic period, when the Dura Europos synagogue was built, resurrection of the dead was a literal belief. Rabbi Yochanan, who lived in the third century, requested that he be buried in clothes that were neither black nor white, since he didn't know whether he would be standing with the righteous or the wicked at the final judgment after his resurrection. When the Talmud spoke of "the world to come" (*olam ha-ba*) it is an interesting historical question as to whether it was generally referring to the eschatological world Rabbi Yochanan anticipated or to the now more familiar concept of a disembodied afterlife.

READING DON DELILLO'S *Zero K*, which came out this spring, got me thinking about resurrection. The novel is about a damaged, diffident middle-aged man named Jeffrey whose father, Ross Lockhart, is a world-bestriding billionaire. Lockhart funds a secret compound where, to quote Scribner's copy, "death is exquisitely controlled and bodies are preserved until a future time when biomedical advances and new technologies can return them to a life of transcendent promise."

The compound, with its "blind buildings, hushed and somber, invisibly windowed," in an undisclosed desert location is somewhere between Google headquarters and the secret desert lair of a Bond villain. Its inhabitants, who include a depressed monk and a philosophical Jew named Ben Ezra (an allusion to Robert Browning's poem), are somewhere between fellows of a think tank, say the Santa Fe Rand-Hartman Institute, and members of a New Age cult. Lockhart's younger second wife Artis has terminal cancer and is preparing to die, or rather to enter a technologically-controlled limbo between life and death while awaiting revival. Ross has brought the skeptical Jeffrey here to say goodbye to his stepmother, and perhaps to him as well.

"The body will be frozen. Cryonic suspension," he said.
"Then at some future time."
"Yes. The time will come when there are ways to counteract the circumstances that led to the end. Mind and body are restored, returned to life."
"This is not a new idea. Am I right?"
"This is not a new idea. It is an idea," he said, "that is now approaching full realization."

Jeffrey's question is about earlier crackpot versions of cryonics ("'People enroll their pets,' I said."), but DeLillo is well aware of the ancient resonance of this idea. Lockhart says:

"Faith-based technology. That's what it is. Another god. Not so different, it turns out, from some of the earlier ones. Except that it's real, it's true, it delivers."

"Life after death."

"Eventually, yes."

"The Convergence."

"Yes."

"The Convergence" sounds like DeLillo's version of futurologist Ray Kurzweil's "Singularity," when, in the very near future, we will transcend "our version 1.0 biological bodies."

DeLillo has always had an apocalyptic streak (*"Everybody wants to own the end of the world"* are the italicized first words of the novel), but what interests me more than his apocalypticism is his attempt to think through what it would really mean for a person to imagine, hope, and plan for an actual bodily resurrection. One of the compound's philosophico-scientific gurus is speaking:

"The dormants in their capsules, their pods. Those now and those to come."

"Are they actually dead? Can we call them dead?"

"Death is a cultural artifact, not a strict determination of what is humanly inevitable."

... "We will colonize their bodies with nanobots."

"Refresh their organs, regenerate their systems."

To plan for resurrection is to believe that one—at least if one is a billionaire—need never succumb to that final winter, that it will be possible for memory, technology, and desire to stir those dull human roots ("Enzymes, proteins, nucleotides") with spring rain and revive the dead.

On the whole, the life after death of *Zero K* is a real resurrection, a promise that revived bodies will emerge from their capsules; it is an Ezekiel-Kurzweilian vision. However, like the actual futurologists, whom DeLillo has apparently studied closely, his characters sometimes offer a different vision of human life 2.0. This is a vision of a disembodied mind that can be downloaded and preserved in any number of substrates; as long as the software and content are preserved, the hard—or wet—ware is a matter of indifference. The tension between these ideas, the world to come in which we have and need our bodies and the world to come in which we don't, is also not new.

It was, in fact, the distinction between an embodied and a disembodied afterlife that animated one of the greatest theological controversies of medieval Judaism. In his *Commentary to the Mishnah*, Maimonides included the resurrection of the dead as one of the thirteen principles of faith. But his purely spiritual account of the world to come, where, to quote one of his favorite Talmudic passages, "there is no eating and no drinking . . . and the righteous . . . bask in the radiance of the *Shekhina*," seemed to make such a resurrection pointless. If one is already a bodiless spirit communing with the divine intellect in an endless seminar on physics and metaphysics, and this is the summit of human attainment, why would one want to be re-encumbered with a body? And how could one's body be revived anyway, given Maimonides' scientific assertion that decay and decomposition are natural and inevitable processes?

Maimonides had an answer for this, albeit one that was unsatisfying and arguably insincere (at least his opponents thought so). An omnipotent God, who can perform miracles, can and will revive the dead in the messianic era, because He promised that He would do so. But then they will die again and return to their superior bodiless existence. In short, spring will return one final glorious time, and then disappear forever. If Maimonides had walked into the Dura Europos synagogue, he probably would have walked right back out again.

Such an austere vision of the afterlife would be wintry comfort for Ross and Artis Lockhart, who, for all their hubris, simply do not want to lose—and can't really imagine losing—their bodies, and hence their selves.

Says Who? Peter Berger's Secret

IN 1990, JUST BACK from studying in Jerusalem for a year, I talked my way into a miserable job in the Los Angeles office of a major Jewish organization. I was called an assistant director of something or other, but my actual duties, such as they were, seemed to consist in helping my boss raise funds to cover his salary and the overhead, and writing a superfluous newsletter, in which I struggled to find the nonexistent sweet spot between synagogue announcements and corporate press releases. We worked in a dingy office on Fairfax that Philip Marlowe might have previously occupied (I could have used his drawer flask). There was a modeling agency, or so it claimed, on the first floor, a kosher pizza parlor down the street, and a sweet old barber named Nathan Newman around the corner who had grown up in the famous town of Mezheritch and survived more than one concentration camp.

One of the things about having a truly bad job is that you find yourself not just bored but needing to remind yourself who you are. I had picked up a little green paperback copy of Peter Berger's *The Sacred Canopy: Elements of a Sociological Theory of Religion* to do just that. On my lunch hours I read dense, nourishing bits of it, puzzling over Germanic formulations such as "Man, as we know him empirically, cannot be conceived of apart from the continuous outpouring of himself into the world in which he finds himself. . . . Human being is externalizing in its essence and from the beginning." (In the margins, I scribbled, "Read Hegel!"—probably still a good idea.) But Berger could also hit you with an epigrammatic little dart: "Religion," he wrote, "is the audacious attempt to conceive of the entire universe as being humanly significant."

In *The Sacred Canopy* Berger argues that the modern state and economy require social spaces and institutions that are free, or mostly free, from the domination of religion and its symbols. In this connection, he liked to quote the seventeenth-century Dutch jurist Hugo Grotius, who said that if international law was to be effective between states with different established religions, it must be framed "as if God did not exist." And as between states, eventually, so too within them; thus, modern workers had to leave their religion at the factory gates. Or, to quote the famous advice from the poet Yehudah Leib Gordon to his fellow nineteenth-century Jews: "Be a man in the streets and a Jew at home." But—and this returns us to Berger's Hegelian point—if you get used to leaving your religion at home, you end up thinking secular thoughts, which leads to the further decline of religion.

This process of secularization inevitably forces religions to enter the marketplace to compete for adherents, but the experience of different options on the consumer side inevitably relativizes the absolute claims of religion. Meanwhile, on the producer side, religious institutions must rationalize themselves along modern, corporate lines in order to effectively compete in the modern world.

These points were not all original to Berger. But he brought them together in a persuasive intellectual package that, unlike the accounts of some of his fellow postwar "secularization theorists," fully recognized the depth of religion. In fact, in a move he owed to Max Weber, he argued that the seeds of this secularization lay not only in the modern reorganization of society but in religion itself—or at least the Bible's original uncompromising rejection of Near Eastern polytheism and, closer to home, the Protestant disenchantment of medieval Christianity. Moreover, as he periodically made clear, while this was his value-free sociological analysis, Berger was himself a serious Protestant who still found what he called "signals of transcendence" in our doubly-disenchanted world.

WHEN I GOT TO Harvard for graduate school, I called up Berger at his Boston University office. Eagerly, I told him that I had read his work closely and that I was planning to write a dissertation on the Jewish Enlightenment, which I wanted to discuss with him. "Well," he said, "you do know that I am not Jewish . . ." I was a bit nonplussed. Here was this giant of social theory, who sometimes used Jewish examples to illustrate his points, and yet he seemed to be suggesting that the fact that he wasn't Jewish disqualified him from discussing an academic topic in Jewish studies. I scrambled for an answer and ended up delivering a presumptuous little lecture on how his theory of secularization applied to the Jewish case, but of course he knew this. After all, hadn't he written at the very conclusion of *The Sacred Canopy* that "the fundamental option between resistance and accommodation must be faced by Judaism, particularly in America, in terms that are not too drastically different from those in which it is faced by the Christian churches"?

Berger listened patiently, and then he said, "You can come to see me, but"—and here he spoke with heavy emphasis—"it sounds like you have read my books . . . and I *haven't thought of anything new.*" That remark did its work. I never forgot it, and I didn't call Berger for another twenty years, though I did think that I saw him once on the Green Line at the Copley station, looking more or less as he had on the back cover of *Facing Up to Modernity*: bald, with a brown cigarillo, like a bookie lost in thought.

As it happens, just a few years later Berger actually did think of something new. As he charmingly tells the story in his introduction to *The Desecularization of the World: Resurgent Religion and World Politics*, his reconsideration of his old theory crystallized when a massive volume called *Fundamentalisms Observed* landed on his desk:

> The Fundamentalism Project was very generously funded by the MacArthur Foundation . . . The book was very big . . . the kind that could do serious injury. So I asked myself, why would the MacArthur Foundation shell out several million dollars to support an international study of religious fundamentalists? Two answers came to mind. The first was obvious and not very interesting. The MacArthur Foundation is a very progressive outfit; it understands fundamentalists to be anti-progressive; the Project, then, was a matter of knowing one's enemies. But there was also a more interesting answer. "Fundamentalism" is considered a strange, hard-to-understand phenomenon; the purpose of the Project was to . . . make it more understandable. But to whom? *Who* finds this world strange? Well, the answer to *that* question was easy: people to whom the officials of the MacArthur Foundation normally talk, such as professors at elite American universities. And with this came the aha! experience. The . . . Project was based on an upside-down perception of the world, according to which "fundamentalism" (which, when all is said and done, usually refers to any sort of passionate religious movement) is a rare, hard-to-explain thing. But . . . [t]he difficult-to-understand phenomenon is not

Iranian mullahs but American university professors—
it might be worth a multi-million-dollar project to try to
explain that!

Berger had once remarked that sociology asks the nervy
little question "*Says who?*" and now he asked it of his colleagues and himself. Not only hadn't the world secularized
in the way that he had thought it would, but the religions
that were resurgent weren't the kind that had made peace
with modernity. Instead, "movements with beliefs and
practices dripping with reactionary supernaturalism (the
kind utterly beyond the pale at self-respecting faculty parties) have widely succeeded." Modernity, Berger went on to
argue, does lead to pluralism, and pluralism does tend to
relativize religious belief, but it hasn't led to a thoroughly
secular world, nor will it. As soon as one stepped out of
the faculty lounge, Berger said, one saw that people moved
from the enchanted groves of tradition to the iron cage of
modern rationality and back again more easily than Max
Weber, or indeed he, had ever thought possible.

IN 2012, I finally got back in touch with Berger. By then, I
was editing the *Jewish Review of Books*, and I wanted him to
write for me. His email back was not quite as discouraging
as our phone call twenty years earlier, but it was not dis-
similar: "I'm not looking for new places to publish (having,
as you know, already contributed greatly to the deforesta-
tion of the planet)—also, I'm over-burdened with work—
also (though this may not be relevant, since you describe
the publication as 'catholic, as it were, in its interests and
approaches'), *I'm not Jewish.*"

Eventually, I prevailed upon him to review Michael Walzer's latest book, *The Paradox of Liberation: Secular Revolu-
tions and Religious Counterrevolutions.* It was obviously right
up his alley, since Walzer's paradox was that religion had

returned with a vengeance to countries like Israel that had been founded by radical secularists. By this time, I also understood his sensitivity about not being Jewish, because I now knew that in fact he was—or rather that he had been born to Jewish parents in Vienna, in 1929. A recent book called *The New Sociology of Knowledge: The Life and Work of Peter L. Berger* by Michaela Pfadenhauer had crossed my desk, and, in her introduction, she briefly sketched Berger's early years, based upon a German memoir he had published in 2008. From Pfadenhauer I learned that Berger and his parents had converted just before fleeing the Nazis in 1938, eventually ending up in British Mandate Palestine. She also wrote that Berger had been hesitant to publish the memoir, even in German, because some of his "Jewish friends might feel snubbed by . . . a decision against a Jewish identity on his part."

Peter and I bantered on the phone and through email while we worked on the Walzer review. I didn't ask him how his life experience related to his sociological theory of religion, though I couldn't help but wonder. Twice, I came close. The first time was when he included a joke about speaking Yiddish in Israel in his piece. The second was when he excitedly told me that he had been invited to address the German Protestant Assembly, and I almost told him the one about the Jewish convert who is invited to give the Sunday sermon and begins, "My fellow goyim . . ." It would have been presumptuous (again), but he probably would have laughed. He enjoyed telling Jewish jokes more than most Lutherans I have known.

Several months later, I visited him at his apartment in Brookline. It had been a hard year. His beloved wife and intellectual collaborator Brigitte Berger had passed away, and he himself was wheelchair-ridden and not well. But he did want to talk. We continued our conversations about religion, doubt, and moderation, and about books on which we agreed and disagreed (including his), and he told me the story of his early life.

His parents were both assimilated Viennese Jews. In 1938, they had gone with a nine-year-old Peter and some other family members to an Anglican cleric who was converting Jews in order to help them flee Austria for a small fee. The conversion was perfunctory. In his memoir *Im Morgenlicht der Erinnerung: Eine Kindheit in turbulenter Zeit* (In the Dawn of Memory: A Childhood in a Turbulent Time), he wrote that his uncle leaned over "and said with a cynical grin, 'So now you are baptized!' I remember how terribly embarrassed I was and I felt somehow humiliated." From there, they went to family in Monfalcone, near Trieste, but they soon realized that they wouldn't be able to stay in Mussolini's Italy. A sympathetic official at the English consulate finally relented when his mother burst into tears, and offered to give them papers to either Kenya or Palestine.

They chose Palestine, because, his mother said, it seemed "less alien," but when they arrived in Haifa they remained Christians, sending Peter—Ya'akov on the Hebrew-speaking street—to a Swiss missionary school. When he was old enough for high school, his schoolteacher took him and two other "Hebrew Christians" to the famous Beit Sefer ha-Reali, but they were rejected by the headmaster as being potentially subversive (*"ein zersetzendes Element"*), which, Peter said, was the *second* time he had heard himself being rejected on such grounds by a representative of the majority. Instead, he went to St. Luke's Anglican School, where most of his teachers were former Jews. At St. Luke's, he was given free rein of the theological library left by a certain Pastor Berg who had returned to Germany. In these years he became a fervent, if, as he later recognized, very idiosyncratic, Lutheran "without ever having met one." After the war, the Bergers left for America as soon as they could. At one point in our conversation, he remarked with some wonder, but no regret, that, had things gone slightly differently, he might have become an Israeli Jew rather than an American Protestant. His English-language memoir, *Adventures of an Accidental Sociologist: How to Explain the World Without Becoming a Bore*, begins his story with his arrival in America and never mentions any of this, though it does have a Jewish joke on the first page.

I thought about my conversation with Peter often in the months that followed, and I sometimes wondered whether I could get him to write about his years in Haifa and their bearing on his later thought, but I never quite got up the nerve. He passed away in 2017, at the age of eighty-eight, having done as much to illuminate the place of religion in the modern world as anyone in the last century. Although none of the obituaries I read seemed aware of Berger's Jewish background, I wasn't the only one who had noticed.

The Committee for the Study of Religion at the CUNY Graduate Center held a memorial conference for him. Its organizer, Samuel Heilman, had studied with Berger at the New School for Social Research in the late 1960s, but he hadn't known his teacher's history until Alan Brill told him about it after Berger's death. In Heilman's perceptive talk, he described the central theme of Berger's work as the way in which in the modern world one's personal identity is determined by choice rather than fate, and persuasively interpreted Berger's German memoir in that light. In Brill's talk, he told us that Rabbi Alexander Schindler, the longtime president of the Union of American Hebrew Congregations, had once consulted Berger about whether the Reform movement should seek converts. The great sociologist replied that it might as well, since all denominations must compete in a pluralist world. Needless to say, Schindler did not ask the nervy follow-up question: *Says who?*

A Short, Angry Talk About
Anti-Semitism on Campus

ABOUT THIRTY-FIVE YEARS ago a writer named George Trow wrote a long, crazy-brilliant, and semi-prophetic essay for the *New Yorker* called "Within the Context of No Context," which described in many ways the world we live in now. When, for instance, Donald Trump, who is apparently on his way to the Republican nomination, describes his incoherent foreign policy as "America First," and the troubling history of that phrase registers as, at best, a passing footnote in the national conversation, then we are living in the context of no context. Much closer to home, when an Oberlin humanities professor—of rhetoric, no less!—repeats on Facebook variations of classic paranoid anti-Jewish fantasies in which sinister, all-knowing, all-powerful Jewish bankers and Israeli spymasters manipulate world events, plan mass murders (including those of fellow Jews), dictate terms to world leaders, and use the Holocaust (which may or may not have happened) as a political tool, and Oberlin as an institution and a community has trouble forthrightly responding to these statements or even saying what they *are*, then we are living in the context of no context. Finally, when the college administration convenes a panel to discuss anti-Semitism without specifying why it is doing so, restricts each speaker to five-to-seven minutes, and then schedules the discussion on the Tuesday evening of finals week, well, then we are speaking in the context of as little context as the college can get away with.

So, time and deans notwithstanding, let me try to address Professor Karega's anti-Semitism as directly as possible. I do not know the professional or legal status of Facebook posts, though they certainly are not private speech, especially if one has colleagues and students who are Facebook friends. But I am clear about two things:

1.) I would not trust the writer of those posts to teach a fair or informed unit on "Israel/Palestine" in, say, her Writing for Social Justice course.
2.) Picking up some neo-Nazi memes and commenting on them approvingly is not academic research, so discussion of academic freedom is a red herring.

To pretend otherwise, to pretend that one can write such things and then walk in and teach an unbiased, intellectually rigorous course, or that somehow these posts are part of a sophisticated research program, and once one properly understands "positionality," and, say, some version of outsider epistemology . . . well, then it will all make sense . . . to pretend, in short, that maybe anti-Semitism isn't anti-Semitism after all, or that it's somehow incidental—just an excess of justifiable anti-Zionist zeal—is to live *in the context of no context.*

Now, one way to describe what we do in the Humanities is to say that we try to understand texts, actions, events by putting them in relevant contexts. In my op-ed piece in the *Oberlin Review,* I laid out some of the historical context of Professor Karega's remarks, which wasn't hard since they were unremarkable, if hateful, instances of modern anti-Semitic rhetoric, which has a 200-year history, and, of course, a theological backstory. But the more important thing to understand is *not* how one Oberlin professor ended up discovering the uniquely inhuman perfidy of the Rothschilds, the Mossad, aged Holocaust survivors, and, of course, Zionists, but how Oberlin has responded this semester—and how it has failed to respond. We are assembled here in Dye Hall, after all, at the very end of the semester after classes have ended, to discuss the matter without exactly discussing the matter.

So in the remaining few minutes that Dean Raimondo has allotted me, let me rapidly sketch—or at least gesture at—three relevant contexts, which I believe we will have to understand if we are to actually learn from this semester. Let's call the first context *Campus-Social*, the second *Political-Ideological*, and the third *Curricular*.

With regard to the campus, let me tell you a story. About ten years ago, a student of mine in her first or second year sat down to lunch at the end of the semester. Two acquaintances came by and sat down at the table with her. One of them asked her what she was doing that summer, and she said that she was going to Israel—at which point both of her would-be friends got up without a word, stared briefly at her, and left. There were no questions asked, no difficult discussions of inconvenient facts, complex history, political theory; certainly no invitation to hear why she was going or what she thought. And I doubt very much, by the way, that it was spontaneous; rather, it was a planned act of public shunning meant to enforce an orthodoxy, a dogma. It was an ugly moment (and one which would never have happened if my student had been going to, say, Pakistan or China or Belarus), and, unfortunately, it was an Oberlin moment.

Let's move quickly to the *Political-Ideological* context. At Oberlin, we like to think of ourselves as unique—long before the silliness of the "We are Oberlin: Fearless" marketing campaign, there was one about our uniqueness— but this campus's irrational obsession with Israel is not unique. It has been a problem of the progressive left for at least fifty years and its roots are demonstrably older than that. The British Labour Party under Jeremy Corbyn is presently tearing itself apart because some of its members have difficulty distinguishing between legitimate criticism of the government of Israel and eliminationist rhetoric which often—and entirely uncoincidentally—dips into the deep historical well of anti-Jewish hatred. This is a subject worthy of critical historical inquiry, though I cannot remember it being discussed on our campus anytime recently.

Which brings us to the third context: *Curricular*. A college catalog is a snapshot of the knowledge the institution as a collective entity thinks is worth having. And yet, as a puzzled colleague recently pointed out to me, there is rarely, if ever, a course on the history and society of Israel from a member of the permanent faculty who has expertise in the subject. Given our evident interest in Israel, such a course might provide needed context.

But at the moment, here at Oberlin, we too often speak and act in the context of no context.

Oberlin and the Illiberal Arts, or Ideological Perversity in Ohio

I WENT BACK to Oberlin on a Friday in June of 2019 for the first time in a year or so. Even retired professors like me have to return books to the library (eventually). Driving off the Ohio-10 freeway, down East Lorain Street, past the organic George Jones Farm—named for a beloved botany professor, not the great country-and-western singer—I saw the first of several yard signs supporting Gibson's Bakery in its lawsuit against Oberlin College and its dean of students, Meredith Raimondo, who is also vice president of the college. The previous day, a Lorain County jury had awarded Gibson's an astounding $33 million in punitive damages in addition to the $11.2 million it had already assigned to the family business for compensatory damages.

The jury found that Oberlin College and its dean of students had maliciously libeled the Gibson family as racists, deliberately damaged their business, by suspending and later canceling its century-long business relationship with the bakery—all while unofficially encouraging a student boycott. The jury also found that the college had intentionally inflicted emotional distress on the Gibsons themselves.

At least neither Dean Raimondo nor anyone in the Oberlin administration were found to have harmed the Gibson family dog. But someone did slash the tires of their employees' cars; there were anonymous threats; and someone harassed the ninety-year-old paterfamilias, Allyn W. Gibson, in the middle of the night, causing him to slip and crack three vertebrae. All because on November 9, 2016, his grandson and namesake Allyn Gibson, who is white, had caught an underage African American student named Jonathan Aladin first trying to buy and then trying to steal wine from the store with two college friends. When Gibson tried first to call the police and then to take a picture of Aladin with two bottles of wine under his shirt, Aladin slapped the phone out of his hands and ran out of the store. Gibson chased him across the street, tried to stop him, and was beaten up by Aladin and his friends. "I'm going to kill you," Gibson reported Aladin saying. Aladin and his friends, Endia Lawrence and Cecelia Whettstone, were arrested. The Gibsons pressed charges against the students despite the college's repeated demands that they drop them.

In court, Raimondo and other key players in the Oberlin administration were shown to have actively supported two days of student protests against Gibson's after the arrests, cursed and derided the Gibson family and its supporters in emails and texts—"idiots" was among the milder epithets—and ignored those within the college who urged deliberation, compromise, and restraint. Oberlin President Marvin Krislov and others rejected the Gibson family's repeated pleas to renounce the charge that they were racists, even when presented with strong statistical and anecdotal evidence that this was not the case.

In August 2017, nine months after his arrest, Jonathan Aladin pled guilty to misdemeanor charges of attempted theft, aggravated trespassing, and underage purchase of alcohol. His friends pled guilty to the first two charges. All three students read statements to the court acknowledging that Allyn Gibson had been within his rights to detain them and that his actions had not been racially motivated. On the sidelines of the court, the director of Oberlin's Multicultural Resource Center and interim assistant Dean of Students, Antoinette Myers, texted her supervisor, Dean Raimondo. "After a year,"—that is, after the students were eligible to have their criminal records expunged—"I hope we rain fire and brimstone on that store," Myers wrote.

The fact that the students' guilty plea was the result of a plea deal, as most criminal convictions are, and that the students' allocution was compelled by the court (a feature of criminal justice with deep roots in common law) encouraged many students and faculty to believe that *somehow* this had still been a racist incident. How, exactly, was never made clear. What should Allyn Gibson have done with an underage customer who had just shown him a clearly fake I.D. and now had two bottles of wine under his shirt? Perhaps if Gibson had said something like "Come let us reason together: I can't sell you wine but I can share a nice cold Snapple with you while we discuss my family's exceedingly thin profit margins and how we are both oppressed under Neoliberalism," things would have been different. They might even have found out that they had something in common, since Jonathan Aladin was the student treasurer at Oberlin, which also has thin margins.

In the fall of 2017, Roger Copeland, a distinguished professor of the history of theater, wrote in to the student paper. The college's stance toward Gibson's, he said, had been "evocative of the topsy-turvy value system in *Alice's Adventures in Wonderland*, wherein the Red Queen declares,

'Sentence first—verdict afterward.'" Now that an actual legal verdict was in, he urged the students, faculty, and administration to accept it:

> The facts of this case are no longer in question. And yet, a counter-narrative has taken hold, one that refuses to allow mere "facts" to get in the way. . . . At what point do you accept the empirical evidence, even if that means having to embrace an "inconvenient" truth? . . . The time has come for the Dean of Students, on behalf of the College, to apologize to the Gibson family for damaging not only their livelihood but something more precious and difficult to restore—their reputation and good standing in the community.

Copeland's letter was headlined "Gibson's Boycott Denies Due Process." He wasn't wrong about the boycott. As the student editor of another campus publication wrote that fall, addressing new students, "the social implications of being seen at Gibson's are much worse than any freshman *faux pas* I can imagine."

But it was Copeland's letter that upset administrators. Upon reading it, Oberlin's Vice President of Communications Ben Jones texted Meredith Raimondo the following: "FUCK ROGER COPELAND!" To which Raimondo responded, "Fuck him. I'd say unleash the students if I wasn't convinced this needs to be put behind us." Which is to say, if prudence hadn't suggested otherwise at that moment, Oberlin's dean of students thought it would be a good idea to incite students against a professor for urging a respect for facts, law, and the welfare of one's neighbors.

Copeland knew something about unleashed students and summary social justice on campus. Three years earlier, he had had a sharp exchange with a student during the rehearsal of a play and ended up being investigated for "a

possible violation of Title IX," the civil-rights law that prohibits discrimination in education based on sex. He was
directed to sign a document acknowledging the complaint,
though he was not allowed to know his accuser or the
details of the complaint. In what is perhaps the best-known
line of a widely read *New Yorker* article about radical politics at Oberlin, Copeland told author Nathan Heller that he
had thought "I'm cast in one of my least favorite plays of all
time, 'The Crucible' by Arthur Miller!" Raimondo was in
charge of Title IX enforcement at the time. When Copeland got a lawyer, the complaint evaporated. (After reading
the crude texts about him, the Gibsons, and others from
erstwhile colleagues, one wonders if Copeland now thinks
Oberlin might be closer to Mamet than Miller. Call it "Ideological Perversity in Ohio.")

Copeland wasn't the only professor urging reconciliation
now that the Gibson's version of events had been unambiguously vindicated. Booker Peek, a longtime professor
of education and Africana studies who heads a program in
which Oberlin students tutor students in the local school,
lamented the rift between the town and the college, and
urged an out-of-court settlement, noting that Gibson's had,
"to its credit, [done] all that it could to keep the matter from
ever going to trial in the first place." Appealing to history,
he reminded his readers that the Gibson family had come
to Oberlin in the nineteenth century because of their opposition to slavery. Moreover, "a bare-knuckled, nasty, public
fight will leave ugly scars and a putrid smell with no true
winner." Meanwhile, Kirk Ormand, a professor of classics,
urged the administration to address the problem of student
shoplifting more seriously. "I'm so sick of Kirk," Dean Raimondo wrote to her colleagues.

So, how exactly, did a famously liberal liberal arts college
end up looking and acting like the arrogant, small-minded,
vindictive corporation in a second-rate John Grisham novel?

Turning from East Lorain on to College Street with its spreading old elm and maple trees, I put that question out of my mind and thought instead of the quirky, talented, sometimes brilliant students I had taught at Oberlin for eighteen years, from 2000 until my retirement in 2018. There was the scholarship kid from Indianapolis who ended up clerking on the D.C. Circuit, the violinist who became obsessed with how Maimonides cited scripture, the girl from rural Minnesota who understood Spinoza better than anybody else, the neo-Hasidic defensive lineman, the kid from Cameroon who compared the Talmudic law of lost objects to the oral traditions his mother had memorized. . . . Oberlin students were rarely as disciplined as the intimidating academic thoroughbreds I had briefly taught at Stanford, but they were often more interesting. They had come to Oberlin, literally, *out of curiosity*.

So, to reframe the question: How does an institution take kids like *that*, and, by precept and example, teach them to rush to judgment, ignore evidence, disdain the legal system, and demonize neighbors who are different? On that last point—that of *difference*, as we say in the academy—Dean Raimondo went to Brown and Emory, President Krislov had been a Rhodes Scholar, Jonathan Aladin had come to Oberlin from Phillips Andover.

Allyn Gibson? He's a fifth-generation townie.

Oberlin doesn't run summer sessions, so there weren't many students in town when I drove in, but there were a lot of middle-aged folks on College Street with nametags and shopping bags. It looked like an alumni event, but it turned out to be the annual conference of the Socialist Workers Party—the Trotskyite group that broke with the Communist Party during the 1930s Stalinist show trials. When I walked into Gibson's there was an unusually large stack of the local newspaper, *The Chronicle Telegram*, with the headline "Gibson's total award: $44M." Along with Gibson's chocolates and locally famous whole-wheat donuts, the Socialist Workers were buying up souvenir copies of the newspaper and congratulating the cashier on the victory. They seemed not to have gotten Oberlin's progressive memo about Gibson's—or rather to have rejected it. "This was always bullshit," a demure woman with a SWP name-etag said. "I've been coming to Gibson's for years, they're good people."

I've also been coming to Gibson's for years. When I interviewed for a job at Oberlin two decades ago, one of my faculty hosts, who, like many professors, was himself an Oberlin graduate, took me by the store, rhapsodized about those whole-wheat donuts, and bought me one of the Gibson's postcards they still have up by the cash register. It's an undated picture of the storefront in the twilight after a light snow and looks like it could have been taken any time since the 1930s (the store was founded in 1885 and has been at its current location since 1905). Allyn W. Gibson, who must have been about seventy at the time, rang up the sale. Walking around the store now, I was struck by how sparsely the shelves were stocked, and wondered if it was a result of the student boycott. I bought three postcards, a Snapple, and a copy of the paper.

The *Chronicle Telegram* has followed the Gibson's case from the outset, with detailed reporting from Scott Mahoney, Dave O'Brien, and Jodi Weinberger. Cornell Law School professor William Jacobson has also discussed it from the beginning on his *Legal Insurrection* blog, along with local freelance reporter Daniel McGraw, who covered every day of the trial in great detail for *Legal Insurrection*. While following the case as a former Oberlin professor was depressing, reading all of these excellent, unpretentious journalists as they chronicled the conduct of local police officers, attorneys, and judges, calmly ascertaining facts and administering justice, was restorative.

The Gibson's v. Oberlin College story is about campus politics. As such, it is frequently ridiculous. But insofar as it shows in stark, petty detail the ideologically driven failures of deliberation and judgment, the craven political calculations, and the cynical abuses of power in an institution ostensibly devoted to higher learning, it is instructive.

Robert Caro, the great biographer of LBJ and Robert Moses, famously wrote that "if you really want to show power in its larger aspects, you need to show the effects on the powerless, for good or ill." Oberlin College has more than one billion dollars in assets, about three thousand students, and several hundred faculty and staff. Gibson's is a small family grocery that has always depended on the college in direct and indirect ways for its business.

Whether the extraordinary verdict against Oberlin will force a cultural reckoning of some kind remains an open question. Oberlin's reputation has certainly suffered, as Professor Peek predicted, and the college has signaled that it will appeal. Immediately after the verdict, current college president Carmen Twillie Ambar wrote to faculty and alumni that it was "just one step along the way of what may turn out to be a lengthy and complex legal process. I want to assure you that none of this will sway us from our core values." Even if the college were to win its appeal on, say, narrow technical grounds, it wouldn't show that the assault on Gibson's was somehow about anyone's "core values," even Oberlin's.

HERE IS what happened.

Although Jonathan Aladin, his friends, and Allyn Gibson are all formally on the record as agreeing on the events in Gibson's on the afternoon of November 9, third-party accounts begin with the Oberlin police arriving a few minutes after the initial contretemps. When Officer Victor Ortiz got there, he later testified, "we saw two young ladies standing over [Gibson] and throwing haymakers . . . The two women would stand over him and kick him, and then crouch down and throw punches. As we got closer, we could see [Gibson] on his back, with the male [Aladin] on top of him and punching him."

The next day, between two hundred and three hundred Oberlin students mounted a protest against Gibson's. They chanted "wake up, stay woke" as they held up hand-lettered signs, some with familiar slogans ("No Justice, No Peace," "Black Lives Matter") and others which specifically called out Allyn Gibson and his family as racists who should be boycotted.

A confident representative of the black student organization, ABUSUA, led chants and danced a little as she read a statement to kick things off:

> We are here today because yesterday three students from the Africana community were assaulted and arrested as a result of a history of racial profiling and racial discrimination by Gibson's Bakery. There is a need for justice to be served to hold Gibson's accountable for its injustices and patterns of unlawful behavior.

She made no mention of shoplifting. Neither did the protest flyers, which had an old-school agitprop aesthetic and read, in part, "This is a Racist establishment with a LONG ACCOUNT [sic] of RACIAL PROFILING and DISCRIMINATION. Today we urge you to shop elsewhere in light of a particularly heinous event involving the owners of this establishment and local law enforcement. PLEASE STAND WITH US," below a starburst with "DON'T BUY" at its center. It also had the following description of the event at Gibson's:

> A member of our community was assaulted by the owner of this establishment yesterday. A nineteen y/o young man

was apprehended and choked by Allyn Gibson . . . the young man who was accompanied by 2 friends was choked until they forced Allyn to let go. After the young man was free, Allyn chased him again until Oberlin police arrived. The three were racially profiled on the scene. They were arrested without being questioned, asked their names or read their rights . . .

The flyers were apparently run off for free on an Oberlin College copier in the nearby Conservatory of Music. Students were told that if they ran out of flyers, they could go back and copy more. The administrative assistant at the Conservatory who helped them was also fairly certain that an assistant dean who worked for Meredith Raimondo had himself run some off during the protest, though he denied it on the witness stand.

One of the principal requirements for proving libel is to show that the defendant has in some sense published the defamatory claims—for instance, by printing hundreds of copies and handing them out at a rally. In his jury instructions, trial judge John R. Miraldi explained that, if the flyer's statements were determined to have been false, that would suggest the flyers were "libelous per se, meaning that they are of such a nature that it is presumed that they tend to degrade or disgrace plaintiffs, or hold plaintiffs up to public hatred, contempt, or scorn [and] . . . injure plaintiffs in their trade or profession." Using Oberlin equipment to make copies of the flyers was a ruinous decision—since no history of racial profiling and discrimination by Gibson's, long or short, was demonstrated in the court, or, for that matter, outside it. Indeed, Oberlin's legal defense implicitly acknowledged this by arguing not that such claims were true but that it had had no part in making them. It was just the students.

And what of the "particularly heinous event" perpetrated by Gibson and the police as described in the flyer? Well, Allyn Gibson's actions in chasing down a shoplifter may have been overzealous or foolhardy (given the beating he took), but they were certainly not heinous. Moreover, police bodycam footage depicted officers calmly going about their business, acting firmly, but avoiding confrontation and collecting evidence, trying to understand what happened. The footage shows Aladin asking the officer why he is being arrested and not Gibson, and the officer responds, "Well, when we got here, you all were on top of him whaling on him." Every statement—every statement—on the protest flyer was false and defamatory.

The protest did not take place on campus, but Dean Raimondo was on hand. Indeed, emails show her calling a staff meeting to prepare for it early that morning. Raimondo and the college maintain that she was merely there to "support" the students in the value-neutral sense of that word. However, accounts of her actions at the rally by several witnesses do not paint the picture of a neutral bureaucrat-observer. Although she at first denied doing so, Dean Raimondo gave a copy of the defamatory flyer to at least one person at the protest—who, unfortunately for her and the college, turned out to be Jason Hawk, editor of the *Oberlin News-Tribune*. She also tried to prevent him from taking pictures. ("Very challenging interaction with guy who says he's a photographer for the Tribune," she texted Director of Communications Scott Wargo.) Hawk testified that he saw her addressing the crowd with a bullhorn to tell them there was free pizza and soda for them provided by the college in the Music Conservatory building across the street. According to a FAQ sheet Oberlin sent to professors and staff after the verdict, Raimondo handled the bullhorn for no more than two minutes, but Rick McDaniel, a former Oberlin College Director of Security, thought she was on the bullhorn for more than twenty minutes. He also testified to being harassed by a college employee when he tried to take pictures.

Trey James, an African-American employee of Gibson's who was working during the protests, testified that he saw Raimondo "standing directly in front of the store with a megaphone. . . . It appeared she was the voice of authority. She was telling the kids what to do, where to go. Where to get water, use the restrooms, where to make copies." As for those flyers, James testified that "she had a stack of them and while she was talking on the bullhorn, she handed out half of them to a student who then went and passed them out." James, a thoughtful, witty man with whom I've chit-chatted over the years, has also forcefully and repeatedly asserted that the Gibsons are not racists, as have other African-American friends and neighbors. During the protests, a shaken Lorna Gibson, Allyn Gibson's mother, was comforted by Vicky Gaines, an African American nurse who grew up in Oberlin and works for the college. Later she told the jury, "I've known them for about forty years, our kids played together, we go to their sporting events, eat at each other's homes, no, never even heard of them thought of as being racist."

Although the mood of the students ranged from boisterous to a kind of glum self-righteousness, there seemed to be very little sense that the Gibsons themselves might be suffering. Student Kameron Dunbar, who was perhaps the most widely quoted of the protesters, instead emphasized how hard the protest was on him.

"Nobody wants to protest. Students don't get joy from waking up in the morning and asking, 'What are we gonna protest next?'" he said. "[These] were some of the most emotionally exhausting days of my life. . . . I think it's easy to essentialize this moment into another 'college kids gone crazy.' . . . For the Oberlin community, this is so serious, and I just wish the broader community was afforded the opportunity to gain the nuance that I have."

Among the "nuances" Mr. Dunbar and his fellow protesters appeared not to get was the relevance of the facts of the case and the financial and emotional stress being inflicted upon an innocent family. A liberal-arts education is often said to teach students how to put themselves in the shoes of their fellow citizens. Suppose that Mr. Dunbar and his friends had thought about what it was like for the Gibsons and their employees to see hundreds of angry students marching out of their castle- and cathedral-like campus buildings and over the massive manicured lawn of Tappan Square to try to destroy their business because they had the temerity to try to stop a shoplifter. (Neither the *New York Times*, nor *Rolling Stone*, nor any of the other media outlets that quoted Dunbar noted that he worked alongside Jonathan Aladin in the Office of the Student Treasurer and was a paid blogger for Oberlin's Office of Communications.)

WHEN IT GOT a little chilly in the evening of the first day of the protests, a student-organizer bought the remaining protesters gloves. Raimondo approved a reimbursement for the gloves the next day.

On the first day of the protest, less than twenty-four hours after the incident, the Oberlin Student Senate passed a resolution that began by saying that as a result of "conversations with students involved, statements from witnesses, and a thorough reading of the police report, we find it important to share a few key facts." It went on:

A Black student was chased and assaulted at Gibson's after being accused of stealing. Several other students, attempting to prevent the assaulted student from sustaining further injury, were arrested and held by the Oberlin Police

Department. In the midst of all this Gibson's employees were never detained, and were given preferential treatment by police officers. Gibson's has a history of racial profiling and discriminatory treatment of students and residents alike. Charged as representatives of the Associated Students of Oberlin College we have passed the following resolution:

... WHEREAS, Gibson's Food Market and Bakery has made their utter lack of respect for the community members of color strikingly visible, therefore be it

RESOLVED that the Students of Oberlin College immediately cease all support, financial and otherwise, of Gibson's Food Market and Bakery; and be it further

RESOLVED that the students of Oberlin College call on President Marvin Krislov, Dean of Students Meredith Raimondo, all other administrators and the general faculty to condemn by written promulgation the treatment of students of color by Gibson's.

As with the protest flyer, virtually every statement here would prove to be misleading, demonstrably false, or aimed at directly harming Gibson's. Indeed, although the student senators made a show of fact-finding, they plainly rejected the police report because it did not tell the story they wanted to hear, and the only witnesses they spoke to were the students hanging out across the street from Gibson's in Tappan Square, not those who were in the store with Allyn Gibson and Jonathan Aladin.

Raimondo was the official advisor to the Student Senate. In that role, she might have advised the senators that it is impossible to discern facts that quickly or with that much certitude—as the study of, say, history, philosophy, politics, literature, and law make plain. She might also have noted that, after all, incidents of student shoplifting at Gibson's were well-known all over town, so it would hardly be implausible that Aladin and his friends had tried to steal some wine and were now denying it. Indeed, as dean of students, Raimondo must have known that two (white) students had been arrested for shoplifting at Gibson's earlier that week.

Or she could have walked the senators from the Wilder Student Union over to the library next door and checked out Roland Baumann's documentary history of black life and education at Oberlin from 1833 to 2007. Despite Oberlin's genuinely admirable history of race relations, Baumann discusses several controversial incidents of discrimination by Oberlin businesses, including segregated barbershops in 1944 and the NAACP's protest against racial discrimination at two lunch parlors after World War II. Gibson's had been an institution in Oberlin for more than fifty years at that point—and its name is conspicuous by its absence from Baumann's history.

Raimondo might also have checked out Charles Homer Haskins' *The Rise of the Universities*, in which it turns out that town-gown conflicts have been about stealing, drinking, and brawling with townies, in particular local shopkeepers, since the Middle Ages. If students of every distinguished university since the founding of the University of Paris had been caught stealing from locals and responded with fists, maybe, just maybe, Raimondo and the student senators might have speculated, this could have been the case here as well. But this was not to be a "teachable moment," or, at any rate, that's not the sort of teaching that was going on.

The defamatory Student Senate resolution was posted in the Student Union building for more than a year. That is to say, it was also, in the legally relevant sense of the word, published. This was also the case for the Department of Africana Studies message on its public Facebook wall, which read: "Very Very proud of our students! Gibson's has been bad for decades, their dislike of Black people is palpable. Their food is rotten and they profile Black students. NO MORE!"

The following day, with the picketing of Gibson's still ongoing, faculty and students received an email from President Krislov:

> Regarding the incident at Gibson's, we are deeply troubled because we have heard from students that there is more to the story. . . . We will commit every resource to determining the full and true narrative, including exploring whether this is a pattern and not an isolated incident. . . . Accordingly, we have taken the following steps: 1) Dean Meredith Raimondo and her team have worked to support students and families affected by these events, and will continue to do so. 2) Tita Reed, Special Assistant for Government and Community Relations, has reached out to Mr. Gibson to engage in dialogue that will ensure that our broader community can work and learn together in an environment of mutual respect free of discrimination.

The letter did not use the word "shoplifting," which Krislov worried in an email to his staff might "trigger" student anger.

Meanwhile, Gibson's supporters were getting a little angry themselves. By the evening of the first protest, people from Oberlin and all over Lorain County, many of whom had grown up going to Gibson's, were coming to support the store and walking out with baked goods, ice-cream cones, and groceries. Bob Frantz, a conservative talk-show host in nearby Cleveland, came and urged his listeners to support Gibson's, and a counter-protest "cash mob" of supportive customers was planned for the coming Saturday. Apparently concerned that the protests were backfiring, a worried Raimondo emailed the Oberlin Student Senators: "At this point, demonstrations are driving u[p] Gibson's business." The Saturday demonstrations were duly canceled, a fact that suggests that Raimondo knew not only how to "unleash the students," but how to re-leash them.

Shortly thereafter, Oberlin's food services canceled its weekly bakery order from Gibson's, under orders from Dean Raimondo. When owner David Gibson (Allyn Gibson's father and the elder Allyn W. Gibson's son) met with representatives of the college, he was told that the order would not be resumed as long as Gibson continued to press charges against the students. The following semester the orders were resumed, though the crippling informal student boycott continued; when Gibson's later filed suit, the orders were canceled again. Emails revealed at the trial showed several members of the Oberlin administration discussing the financial hit Gibson's was taking and speculating on the leverage it gave the college in their attempt to get the charges against Aladin and his friends dropped. A professor of music theory who had been at Raimondo's planning meeting for the student protest wrote of the Gibsons that "they own so much prime property in oberlin [sic] that boycotting doesnt [sic] hurt them that much. The smear on their brand does, and that's been taken care of." In fact, both the boycott and the smear hurt not only the Gibson family but the employees the bakery found itself forced to lay off.

David Gibson brought statistics from the Oberlin Police Department to the college showing that of the forty people arrested for shoplifting at Gibson's over the previous five years, thirty-three were students of the college, thirty-two were white, six were African American and two were Asian, which almost perfectly matched the racial makeup of the city. Despite its stated determination to explore "whether this is a pattern and not an isolated incident," Krislov's administration was unmoved. At trial, the college's lawyers tried and failed to have the statistics quashed as evidence.

Emails, texts, and other evidence that came out in the trial don't paint a picture of a billion-dollar institution full of intellectually accomplished people committing "every resource to determining the full and true narrative." Ben Jones, the head of Oberlin PR who drafted that letter for Krislov, called the police report "bullshit," based on vague rumor and speculation. During the trial Ferdinand Protzman, Krislov's chief of staff, was forced to answer that although neither he nor his colleagues believed the Gibsons to be racists, they also never considered publicly declaring that the Gibsons were not.

As for Raimondo and Tita Reed, who were named as the point persons in finding that "full and true narrative," David Gibson testified that Raimondo warned him that she had sent people door-to-door to ask if the Gibsons were racists. Raimondo denied that in court—but in any event, no such witnesses were produced by Oberlin (truth is, of course, always an absolute defense against libel). While she was ostensibly working on finding the "full and true narrative," Ms. Reed was forwarded an email from an Oberlin employee and resident of the town who wrote:

> I have talked to 15 townie friends who are poc (persons of color) and they are disgusted and embarrassed by the protest. In their view, the kid was breaking the law, period (even if he wasn't shoplifting, he was underage). To them this is not a race issue at all and they do not believe the Gibsons are racist. They believe the students have picked the wrong target . . . I find this misdirected rage very disturbing, and it's only going to widen the gap (between) town and gown.

The college president's special assistant for *community* relations responded: "Doesn't change a damn thing for me."

"OBERLIN IS PECULIAR in that which is good," said John J. Shipherd, one of its nineteenth-century utopian founders, riffing on Paul's epistle to Titus, which, in turn, alludes to God's choice of the people of Israel as his "peculiar treasure," because of the willingness to obey His law. And Oberlin *was* peculiarly good, accepting and graduating students regardless of race or sex from the very beginning, including some of the most academically accomplished women and black Americans of the nineteenth century. It was also an important stop on the Underground Railroad when Charles Grandison Finney, a charismatic leader of the Second Great Awakening of evangelical Christianity, was president of the college.

More than a century after that, long after the biblical resonance of Shipherd's statement was forgotten, there was a campus joke that Oberlin was, instead, "good in that which is peculiar." But the Gibson's episode wasn't even peculiar, it was drearily predictable. In 2013, the administration fell for a racist hoax. A sudden spate of Nazi graffiti and racist flyers caused such hysteria on campus that a student reported seeing a hooded Klansman. Oberlin canceled classes for a day, and held a teach-in against racism in Finney Hall. I remember a first-year girl crying as she spoke, innocently asking, "Is this what it's like here?" Well, yes and no. The local police later suggested that the Klansman was just a student with a blanket draped over her shoulders—or maybe nothing at all. Meanwhile, by the time the college administrators had called off classes, they already knew that the perpetrators were a couple of student trolls with murky, but seemingly liberal, politics, and had quietly removed them from campus. When President Krislov appeared on CNN to extoll the educational value of the day off, students could be heard behind him chanting "Bullshit, bullshit!" Little did they know.

Two years later, students protested "cultural appropriation" in the dining hall: The banh mi sandwich was made with soggy ciabatta, not a crispy baguette, General Tso's chicken was steamed, not fried, and so on. This too made the national media where it was widely noted that banh mi is already a French-Vietnamese mashup, that General Tso's Chicken is an American invention, and that, well, dorm food is . . . dorm food. Later in the fall of 2015, the black student union, ABUSUA, presented the college with an extraordinary fourteen-page list of demands. These included the complete overhaul of the curriculum along prescribed ideological lines, stipends for black student leaders, the immediate or guaranteed promotion/tenuring of nineteen favored professors and administrators, the summary dismissal of no fewer than seven other professors and administrators, designated "safe spaces" for black students, a bridge program for recently released prisoners—the compatibility of these last two demands was not addressed—and much, much more. Krislov summarily rejected the demands to significant national acclaim, but there was grumbling on campus among radical students and a few faculty members. It wasn't that they actually expected the college to implement millennial Maoism, but they might have sensed that this act had depleted the presidential courage bank, and were waiting to see what would happen next.

That spring, an article by David Gerstman in *The Tower. org* revealed that a young African-American assistant professor of rhetoric and composition named Joy Karega was pushing wild anti-Semitic conspiracy theories on Facebook: for instance, that Israel and super-rich "Rothschild-led banksters" were really behind 9/11, the *Charlie Hebdo* attacks, and ISIS. As it happens, Karega was one of the professors singled out for guaranteed insta-tenure in the student demands. President Krislov first issued a terse defense of free speech while noting only that these posts "do not represent the views of Oberlin College." When, as chair of Jewish Studies, I pointed out to him that no one thought that Oberlin held these views, but that a representative of the college ought to be able to say precisely what kind of views they were, he demanded that I clear anything I wrote with his PR man, Ben Jones. I ignored him and began planning my early retirement, though I didn't realize it at the time. The college administration continued to flounder wildly in its response to Karega until a frustrated Board of Trustees took the matter out of their hands and announced her dismissal that fall.

How, after such public debacles costing millions of dollars in lost students, donors, and prestige, could Oberlin yet again condescend to its students, betray its finest traditions, and make itself a national laughingstock? Or as another Oberlin professor put it to me in a pithy email after the Gibson's v. Oberlin verdict, "How idiotic can the college be always?"

If there is one thing that Oberlin's critics and its administration have agreed on, it's the significance of the fact that Jonathan Aladin was caught stealing wine on November 9, 2016—the day after President Trump was elected. Those were extraordinary times in traumatized liberal and left circles, and the college encouraged us to help our students work through their shock. Certainly this was part of what was going on in the Gibson's protest. The small town *petit bourgeois* shop owners were made to stand in for all that was wrong and bewildering in America. But does that really explain the ensuing two-and-a-half years of systematic and unremitting hostility?

IF CAMPUS POLITICS are often ridiculous, they are always local, and the Gibson's initial complaint suggested a set of local reasons for the trouble that were left largely unexplored in the trial and its coverage. Meredith Raimondo had been appointed vice president and dean of students in the midst of the Karega controversy with the specific mandate to "address campus climate, including . . . items identified as high priority by ABUSUA." When the Gibson's protests began, Karega's fate was still officially undecided. But, as Raimondo must have known, and the students did not, the Trustees were going to announce her dismissal in just a few days. There was thus something fortuitous in the distraction provided by this new crisis. Whatever the degree of calculation involved, it proved useful to the administration for activist students to have spent what Kameron Dunbar called "some of the most emotionally exhausting days of my life" in picketing Gibson's little storefront with the solicitous support of college administrators—rather than picketing the graceful sandstone Mediterranean Romanesque Cox Administration building just a couple of hundred yards away. Indeed, as it turned out, the response to Karega's final dismissal the following week was surprisingly muted. Oberlin, one might conjecture, is Machiavellian in that which is politically correct.

And then there was the real estate. Oberlin is a company town. In fact, the college was founded before the town. Recall the music professor's seemingly irrelevant remark that the Gibsons "own so much prime property." That property includes a parking lot behind their store, abutting the Music Conservatory. The Gibsons complained that the parking lot was used by the college as spillover parking, to the detriment of the town businesses, including theirs. This complaint suggested that, like any ruthless monopolist, Oberlin College didn't like competition and wouldn't mind forcing its competitors into the position of having to sell cheap.

Such possible motives suggest that Oberlin College acted like a John Grisham villain because it is one. However, I think there are two other reasons that come closer to the heart of the current crisis over the mission of the university and the nature of a liberal arts education. If Oberlin and Raimondo seem to have treated Oberlin's activist students as a constituency to be manipulated, they also catered to them as customers. And the customer, unlike the student, is always right. When asked why the college could not send out a notice supportive of the Gibsons, Krislov's chief of staff, Ferdinand Protzman, replied that "both the college and Gibson's are dealing with the same customer base," and there was no profit in irritating the most vocal members of that customer base. The college participated in the "smearing of the Gibsons" because, like easy grades and better banh mi sandwiches, it's what the customer wanted. But, of course, real education consists of helping students to see that the most desirable thing is knowledge.

The second and final reason I would suggest begins with an observation: At the height of the protests, no more than ten percent of Oberlin's students were standing in front of Gibson's, even though there is not a lot to do on a week-night in Oberlin, Ohio. Moreover, although an alarming number of administrators, and perhaps a handful professors, were involved in the protests and ensuing conflict with Gibson's, it was an even smaller percentage. There is a kind of modified Pareto principle working at schools like Oberlin in which the radicalized five or ten percent of the population establishes the tone for the entire institution. Of course, this is true of all organizations, but it seems to me that colleges are especially susceptible to this phenomenon precisely because liberal arts education calls out for a unifying principle or goal, something to hold together this four-year experience of 130 credit hours in the history of this and the structure of that. Oberlin, like Cardinal Newman, used to have a theological answer to that question, one which underwrote an impressively principled stand on racial equality in the nineteenth century.

Over the last century, politics replaced theology. "Think one person can change the world? So do we," has been Oberlin's official motto for quite some time. It's just advertising (I remember some campus graffiti from the early 2000s—"Oberlin: changing the world for $30,000/yr"—now it's closer to $60,000). But the attitude expresses the self-image of many liberal arts colleges, and many more professors, and since only radicals "know" how to change the world, it cedes them the high ground. The upshot, at least in this case, has been the furthest thing from idealism possible. Instead of unleashing the potential of students, students were unleashed on an innocent family and business.

I THOUGHT there might be a chance that I would never come back to Oberlin after I dropped by Gibson's and returned my books to the college library, but I couldn't resist browsing in the stacks (it really is an excellent library), and I ended up checking out a little book called *The University of Utopia* by Robert Maynard Hutchins. Writing in 1953, Hutchins (a former Oberlin student and the son and grandson of Oberlin professors) imagined the PR men of the future as secular priests who would point out to their clients not what they could get away with saying but what they *ought* to do. However, such "public duty men" wouldn't be necessary for Utopia's University, because that school's trustees would inevitably hold the university and its professors to live up to their ideals. Hutchins had famously been the president of the University of Chicago, not a comedian at Second City, and his irony was a bit heavy-handed. But he wasn't wrong. A university ought to remember that it is not merely a self-interested corporation but a community of scholars, concerned with truth and convinced that its pursuit is a genuine public good.

Public-spirited utopianism hasn't been much in evidence

in Oberlin's spinning and messaging in the wake of the Gibson's verdict. Before the amount of damages had even been determined by the jury, Oberlin's counsel sent a letter to the faculty expressing disappointment that "the jury did not agree with the clear evidence our team presented," a statement that made her subsequently expressed gratitude for their service sound condescending and insincere. She went on to say that "colleges cannot be held liable for the independent actions of their students . . . [and] are obligated to protect freedom of speech on their campuses." But, of course, what the jury found was that the college had not merely protected freedom of speech on its campus but gone out of its way (and, incidentally, off campus) to defame private individuals. Defamation has never been protected speech. And the First Amendment has certainly never protected the deliberate infliction of financial and emotional harm, which is what the jury decided Oberlin had done.

In the aftermath of the jury's verdict, Krislov's successor as president, Carmen Ambar, along with college proxies and sympathetic journalists, have implied that, guilty pleas, allocutions, and an exhaustive six-week civil trial notwithstanding, there really was, after all, *something* to the claim that Gibson's had racially profiled Aladin and others. In interviews, Ambar has hit on a bit of bad philosophy to obfuscate this point. "You can have two different lived experiences, and both those things can be true," she told the *Wall Street Journal* editorial board. One is tempted to say that the facile relativism of this—there is a Gibson truth and an Aladin truth; a townie truth and a college truth—reveals the sophistry behind Oberlin's self-destructive approach, but actually it's worse than that, if not philosophically, at least morally. Nothing in the actions of Oberlin College or those of its Dean and Vice President suggests an understanding or empathy with the Gibson family's experience.

One thing I didn't know when I wrote this was that David Gibson, the owner of Gibson's Bakery, was dying of pancreatic cancer. He had kept it a secret during the trial, and he passed away just five months after winning that multi-million-dollar judgment. Of course, Oberlin College appealed the decision, and two years after the verdict, his family still had yet to collect.

In November of 2021, I wrote to the Gibson's attorney Lee Plakas, asking for an update. He replied that, although the appeal had been argued a year ago, the Court of Appeals had not yet rendered a decision. Meanwhile, he wrote,

> The continuation of this 135 year iconic family business is in jeopardy. . . . Grandpa Gibson, in his 90s is no longer available to help with business operations. Dave's surviving widow Lorna had vowed to Dave that she would do everything in her power to continue the business, but she may not be able to overcome the continuing actions of the students and the College. . . . In light of the greatly diminished revenues resulting from the lack of business from the College and students, Lorna's only hope was to use the proceeds of the verdict to infuse financial resources to survive the College/student storm. With the delay in payment of the verdict, the storm clouds are darkening.

Earlier in 2021, Oberlin announced that Meredith Raimondo would be stepping down as Vice-President and Dean of Students, and would return to the classroom following a year-long sabbatical.

Nonsense Is Nonsense,
but the History of Nonsense . . .

IN THE SPRING of 1957 Saul Lieberman famously introduced Gershom Scholem's lectures on Merkabah Mysticism at the Jewish Theological Seminary (JTS) by saying "Nonsense is nonsense, but the history of nonsense is a very important science." Lieberman's bon mot has been widely repeated, adapted, and occasionally mangled. It inspired—or perhaps provoked is a better word—a disappointing novel by Chaim Potok and may have been appropriated by the great Harvard philosopher W. V. O. Quine as a curricular motto. It is certainly among the wittiest things ever said in academic Jewish studies, though wit is not, perhaps, our most competitive field.

Scholem, who thought that the Jewish mystical tradition preserved deep and only partially expressible symbolic truths, is unlikely to have been amused, but I know of no direct response on his part. In fact, Lieberman's remark, though often repeated, is itself not perfectly attested. According to the lore which often accompanies its retelling, Lieberman contributed an appendix to the published version of Scholem's lectures by way of apology for the public embarrassment he had caused his friend.

Lieberman's appendix to *Jewish Gnosticism, Merkabah Mysticism and Talmudic Tradition* is a brief and brilliant analysis of mystical rabbinic interpretations of the Song of Songs, but it bears no sign of having served as a means of reconciliation. Lieberman and Scholem had been friends and rivals for a quarter of a century by then, and the appendix seems more like an act of friendly one-upsmanship (that is to say academic collaboration) than an act of atonement. Scholem is invited to Lieberman's academic fiefdom, speaks about previously unrecognized gnostic developments in the heart of the Rabbinic period, and succeeds brilliantly. So Lieberman responds with another set of prooftexts which Scholem hadn't considered.

This rivalry is somewhat heightened in Chaim Potok's *Book of Lights*, where the Lieberman figure is called Kleinman and the Scholem figure is Keter: the "little man" of rationalism and the "crown" of supernal wisdom. Potok was not subtle in his preferences (though, to be fair, there is probably an allusion here to the famous Talmudic statement that the halakhic disputes of Abbaye and Rava are a little thing compared to mysteries of the Divine Chariot). The thematic argument of the novel is that dry rationalism like Lieberman's leads to the atomic nightmare of Hiroshima, while mysticism has the power to heal. (It does not improve in the telling.)

Potok himself was probably not present for Lieberman's joke or Scholem's lectures. He had graduated from JTS several years earlier, served as a chaplain in Korea (the second setting of the novel) and was, at the time, running Camp Ramah in Ojai, California.

Indeed, I have not met anyone who actually attended the lectures, and one might wonder whether Lieberman's introduction is entirely apocryphal. Fortunately, there is a textual version of the witticism. Lieberman repeated the remark in another appendix, one to his classic essay "How Much Greek in Jewish Palestine." There is no reference to Scholem in the text here, but there is a literally subtextual one: the adjacent footnote cites Scholem's lectures on Merkabah Mysticism. So it seems probable that the oral tradition is correct and that Lieberman did say it, and later could not resist publishing it somewhere.

I have also heard the remark attributed verbatim to the great philosopher and logician W. V. O. Quine, meaning here: "Continental philosophy is nonsense, but the history of Continental philosophy is a very important science," or at least not further nonsense. So, if forced to include Heidegger among its course offerings, the department should hire a historian.

This raises two questions, one shallow, the other deep. Let's take care of the shallow one first. Did Quine say it? And if so, did he say it first? Sort of and no. It was certainly his curricular policy to prefer the history of philosophical nonsense to the unmediated stuff. In his philosophical dictionary *Quiddities*, under "Tolerance," he wrote "Scholarship is a matter on which an objective and essentially scientific consensus can prevail, however disreputable its subject matter." But I know of nothing closer than this in print. However, his close Harvard colleague Burton Dreben was widely quoted as saying, "Garbage is garbage but the history of garbage . . . ," which is very close indeed.

Dreben was said to be the only person who knew more about Quine than the great philosopher himself, so it is difficult to distinguish between their respective epigrams. "That is what I said, isn't it, Burt?" Quine is supposed to have said when quoting or clarifying himself in his final years. But we know that Dreben had been married to the daughter of Lieberman's JTS colleague Shalom Spiegel and was familiar with the infamous witticism. So it seems most likely that Quine did indeed make the remark, or something very close to it, though he was not first or even second.

This leaves us, finally, with the deep question. Can one spend a lifetime studying what one believes in the end to be nonsense? Scholem certainly did not think Kabbalah was nonsense, nor, for that matter did Lieberman think that of midrash halakha, though neither of them was quite willing to straightforwardly affirm the metaphysical propositions of their textual subjects either. This question abides.

Wit, I can imagine a reader wearily replying to all this, is wit, but the history of wit is pedantry. Nonsense. Every student of past texts and ideas must contend with the worry that lurks beneath Lieberman's witticism, and we are also obliged to honor our predecessors, our mighty dead, not least by retelling their jokes.

III

Life and Afterlife

Accounting for the Soul

EDITH BROTMAN'S new book *Mussar Yoga*, with its cover photo of a woman in a graceful Tree Pose silhouetted against sea and sky, made me smile when it landed on my desk. Is this, I wondered, the asana for guilt? Because they never stinted on guilt, the old mussarniks. They also renounced Jewish mysticism, paid little attention to their bodies, and even less to other spiritual traditions. So *Mussar Yoga* makes for a surprising deli combo platter of the spirit, even in our easy-going, mix-and-match America.

To be fair, Brotman is aware of the incongruity, more or less. "If you are searching for a pure or traditional approach to *Mussar* or yoga," she writes, "this is not the book for you." And there *is* something to Brotman's idea beyond feel-good American syncretism. The mussar movement attempted to inculcate ethical character traits through a regular practice of disciplined self-reflection, and yoga attempts to do something similar through the body.

In 1844 and 1845 Rabbi Israel Salanter, the founder of the mussar movement, had a publisher in Vilna reprint several works of Jewish ethics, urging both students and laymen to set aside time to study them regularly and apply the lessons to their own lives. One of them was *Cheshbon Ha-nefesh* by Mendel Lefin. The title means, roughly, an "accounting for the soul," and it offers a brilliant method for doing just that. Lefin enumerated thirteen basic virtues and asked the reader to associate each with a short saying or maxim upon which to concentrate. Lefin then instructed the reader to make a simple spreadsheet with the virtues running down the page (one for each week) and the days of the week across the top. So if the reader acted haughtily on, say, Tuesday of week six, when he should have been concentrating on humility (*anava*), he put a black mark in that box. The thirteen virtues (which could be customized) corresponded to the thirteen weeks of a season, so that the reader concentrated on each virtue four times a year.

Cheshbon Ha-nefesh is Brotman's principal model for *Mussar Yoga.* Her list of thirteen virtues is somewhat different (notably missing is Lefin's thirteenth virtue of *perishut*, literally "separateness," roughly speaking, chastity), but the system is the same. Each virtue is now linked to a set of two or three yoga poses. In the place of maxims she introduces mantras that are as likely to derive from the Beatles ("All you need is love") as the Bible ("Love your neighbor as yourself").

Rabbi Salanter probably knew that Mendel Lefin was a modernist when he had *Cheshbon Ha-nefesh* reprinted, but he certainly didn't know that the whole system—thirteen virtues/four yearly cycles, maxims, moral spreadsheets, and all—was cribbed wholesale from Benjamin Franklin's *Autobiography*, which had not yet made its way to religious Jews in the Pale of Settlement. Franklin told his readers that he devised the system after having conceived "the bold and arduous Project of arriving at moral Perfection," which, he cheerfully admitted, turned out to have been harder than he thought. Nonetheless, it really was a brilliant scheme, the first best-selling American self-help system. (In fact, there is now even an app for that "arduous project," called "Ben's Virtues.")

Max Weber famously saw Franklin's system as a secularization of puritan introspection into capitalist productivity. If so, perhaps Salanter unconsciously returned it to its more natural home among the kind of strict pietists who, when faced with temptation, tried to envision the day of their deaths and the punishment that lay beyond.

Not everyone was convinced of the value of mussar. When Salanter's disciple Rabbi Isaac Blazer tried to introduce it into the curriculum of the great yeshiva of Volozhin, Rabbi Hayyim of Brisk rejected the suggestion out of hand. In the famous account of his grandson, Rabbi Joseph Dov Soloveitchik, he replied:

> If a person is sick, we prescribe castor oil for him. . . . [But] if a healthy person ingests castor oil he will become very sick . . . [I]f you are spiritually sick . . . then you must use more powerful drugs . . . the remembrance of the day of death. We in Volozhin, thank God, are healthy . . . If the scholars of Kelm and Kovno feel compelled . . . let them drink to their hearts content, but let them not invite others to dine with them.

One can only imagine the Brisker's response to *Mussar Yoga*, or, for that matter, the response of the mussarniks of Kelm and Kovno. But Ben Franklin probably wouldn't have minded.

ON THE FEW OCCASIONS when I have gone to a yoga class, I've left feeling alert, relaxed, and refreshed—in short, *good*. I've sometimes even had the heretical thought "Why don't I feel this good after shul?" After all, the *Shema* is a meditation on oneness and the *Amida* is a carefully choreographed prayer (three steps forward, three steps back, the necessary bows, the optional swaying). Of course, the problem may be—in fact, certainly is—me. I remember my own brief time in a mussar yeshiva and the elegant intensity with which one particular student would pray, his back ramrod straight, his hands eloquently beseeching. And then, also, the old mussar voice comes back to me: "Who said you were supposed to feel good?"

The Brisker Rav may have been right to reject mussar for Volozhin, and Ms. Brotman may be correct in diluting it for her readers now (though when one reads a mantra like "I love me" one may wonder how much Mussar is left), but it did produce some truly saintly personalities. The main stories about Rabbi Salanter are not about his Talmudic genius or his ritual piety but rather the extraordinary care he took in ordinary interactions: the time on the eve of Yom Kippur he missed Kol Nidre to take care of a stranger's crying baby, the lengths he took to avoid embarrassing recipients of charity, the afternoon he spent trying to lead a lost cow back to its farm, and so on.

One Shabbat, I was playing with my six-year-old daughter Bayla and we started flipping through *Mussar Yoga*. We tried Up Dog, Down Dog, the Boat Pose (a kind of open-armed crunch Brotman for some reason places under Generosity), Reverse Warrior (Humility), and a couple of others. (Incidentally, it turns out that many of the asanas, including the sun salutation exercise, the most common sequence in contemporary yoga, are even more recent than Franklin's *Autobiography*.)

Eventually I pulled something and had to rest in Savasana, the lying-down—literally "corpse"—pose. Lying there, slightly lamed, on my family-room carpet, I remembered the story of Rabbi Salanter's death. He was living alone in Koenigsberg, sick and very poor. Some of his students paid an elderly attendant to stay with him overnight. When they came the next morning, he had passed away.

They asked what his last words had been. The attendant said that Rabbi Israel had spent the night reassuring him that the body of a man was harmless, and that there was nothing to worry about in being alone with a corpse.

Is Repentance Possible?

THE OTHER DAY YouTube decided that I ought to watch a strangely mesmerizing psychologist from Canada named Jordan B. Peterson berate me over my failure to follow his ten rules for success. His first rule was to "stop doing the things that you know are wrong," when you *know* that they are wrong, which is a good, straightforward rule.

It's also a pretty easy one to follow, if you are a robot or an angel. I don't think that Dr. Peterson mentioned that it was Aristotle who first tried to seriously work through the question of how it is that we frequently seem to do things that we know to be against our better judgment. Socrates had said that, although a person may be wrong about what is good for him, "No one goes willingly toward the bad," which seems obviously true until one remembers that, in fact, one does so fairly often. After all, I ought to have tied myself to the mast of Microsoft Word and resisted the siren call of YouTube, whose window I had ostensibly opened in order to . . . well, I am not quite sure what I opened it for anymore, but there must have been a good reason, and it had nothing to do with Jordan B. Peterson or ad words or Google's super-secret distractibility algorithm for middle-aged men.

Akrasia, which is often translated as weakness of the will, is, as Aristotle says in the *Nicomachean Ethics*, a puzzle: If I think that, all things considered, it would be better for me to do Y than X, and I want to do Y more than X, then I will do Y, not X. But sometimes I don't, and you don't; we go on X-ing when our practical reason clearly tells us that we should Y. It is, one might almost say, our natural state to frequently and incontinently X.

In his deep, densely argued new book *Ethics in the Conflicts of Modernity: An Essay on Desire, Practical Reasoning, and Narrative*, Alasdair MacIntyre discusses such an akratic person "who strongly desires something that, so she judges, she has excellent reason not to desire." Perhaps she is tempted to stream a self-help video, which though potentially useful will, nonetheless, derail her from a more important task; but perhaps the stakes are higher, and she is avoiding, say, a difficult but necessary conversation, or choosing a fun but frivolous relationship over a deep one. If she understands her predicament correctly, according to MacIntyre, then she will see that "her predicament is one of desiring a lesser and inappropriate good over a greater and appropriate good." Consequently, MacIntyre writes, "she has every *reason* to redirect" her desires, but reasons alone are not quite enough. Somehow, she must "draw upon the resources provided by her earlier moral training and education and by her present social relationships if she is to act rightly." In short, she must repent, or, as the Jewish tradition has it, "return" to the priorities that she knows are right. MacIntyre writes:

> Aristotle provided an outline account of her situation, partly in what he said about *akrasia* . . . and partly elsewhere. Later Aristotelians, most notably Aquinas, have provided further resources, but the NeoAristotelian account of such conflicts needs further development and

rendering into contemporary terms. Until these have been provided, there is a psychological lacuna in NeoAristotelian theory . . . [but] I see no reason to believe that what is needed cannot be provided.

One wishes that he had provided that theory in this book rather than a suggestive promissory note. But this would be a churlish demand to make of an eighty-eight-year-old philosopher who has helped to reframe the questions of ethics as much as anybody in the last half-century.

Thirty-six years ago, in *After Virtue*, MacIntyre famously argued that modern moral thinking was a mess, a rubble heap of incompatible theories leaving us with an incoherent moral vocabulary in which we appeal to the greatest good for the greatest number at one moment, to rights and duties at another, and to something like transcendent moral law at a third. This left MacIntyre with his famous challenge: Nietzsche or Aristotle? Either morality as we know it should be razed to the ground, or we should junk the implausible systems of what he called "the Enlightenment project" and attempt a qualified return to Aristotle's naturalistic, character-based virtue ethics.

A quarter-century earlier, the Cambridge philosopher Elizabeth Anscombe had suggested that we simply drop "the concepts of obligation, and duty—*moral* obligation and *moral* duty, that is to say—and of what is *morally* right and wrong," and MacIntyre's argument can be taken as filling out Anscombe's suggestion. As Anscombe wrote:

> [T]he *moral* sense of "ought," ought to be jettisoned if this is psychologically possible; because they are survivals, or derivatives from survivals, from an earlier conception of ethics which no longer generally survives, and are only harmful without it.

Anscombe herself was a fervent Catholic, but with the modern eclipse of what she called Judaism and Christianity's "law conception of ethics," she had also recommended a return to Aristotle. MacIntyre himself ended up converting to Catholicism shortly after publishing *After Virtue* (one can see the signs of it already in that book). These are mere biographical facts, but they may make one wonder just how possible it is to do without that moral "ought," and in particular whether precisely that sense of obligation might be one of the necessary resources for the kind of character reform, or repentance, that MacIntyre describes.

ON THE ARISTOTELIAN VIEW, morality is internal to human life rather than a matter of obedience to a set of abstract rules or an external authority. Briefly, we have dispositions to act or react in certain ways, and these dispositions are shaped by education, admonition, example, and habit. The best of these traits will fall between the extremes of behavior: It is bad, for instance, to be either timid or foolhardy, but it is good to follow the "middle path" and be courageous. So, courage is a virtue, and timidity and foolhardiness are vices (though far from the worst ones).

What makes courage and the other virtues—for instance, generosity, truthfulness, and temperance—good is the natural fact that they help a human being to thrive and be happy, in the widest and highest possible sense of that word. Therefore, one ought to develop the virtues because they are, as we now say, "life skills" which will help us succeed, not because we *morally* ought to, in the sense of which Anscombe disapproved. How, exactly, such a system can be, or rather was, adapted to a religion based on divine authority is a question to which I shall return.

In the meantime, however, it's worth noting just how hard a task MacIntyre's akratic woman faces. Her character has been formed by relationships and incidents since birth, many of them forgotten, not to speak of brain chemistry and the blind impress of events. Her actions and desires are, by now, governed by stable habits of action, many of which have been with her since childhood. How likely is it, really, that, in the middle of the journey, she, or any of us, can change these habits, turn vice into virtue? Perhaps this puts the question too strongly, since MacIntyre describes her as a person who is merely tempted by a "lesser and inappropriate good," rather than what is actually bad (the distracting YouTube video or the frivolous friend, not the stiff drink in the afternoon). But, after all, bad desires do happen to good people, even those who have been fortunate enough to grow up with a loving family, good friends, and a well-ordered community.

Aristotle argues that weakness of the will is not quite a vice; it's more, he says, like epilepsy, and, after the temptation has passed, the weak-willed person regrets his actions. But he does not tell us how such regret can be transformed into repentance. As MacIntyre frankly admits, there is a gap, "a psychological lacuna," in the theory, for Aristotle, for his medieval Christian commentator Aquinas, and for us.

As it happens, the Jewish approach to repentance was authoritatively codified by Thomas's great Aristotelian predecessor Moses Maimonides, and his approach demonstrates both the strengths and the weaknesses of virtue ethics, as well, perhaps, as the extent to which moral thinking was messy even before the modern world.

MAIMONIDES ONCE POSED an interesting question which had never occurred to Aristotle (in fact, it wouldn't have made any sense to him), though the Muslim philosopher Alfarabi had earlier asked a similar question for similar reasons. The question is: Who is better, "the man of self-restraint [who] performs moral and praiseworthy deeds," but does so only by struggling with his desires and dispositions, or the man who "acts morally from innate longing and desire" because he has a virtuous character? In this early essay, Maimonides says that philosophers "unanimously agree that [the virtuous man] is superior to, and more perfect than, the one who has to curb his passions," even if they are behaviorally indistinguishable. But, he says, the rabbinic tradition regards the person who must work to subdue his temptation and do the right thing—or stop doing the wrong ones—as better. Among the famous rabbinic sayings he quotes are "the greater the man, the greater his evil inclination," and "according to the difficulty is the reward."

In the end, Maimonides explains away the rabbinic statements that seem to prefer the conflicted man who wrestles with his desires to the virtuous one, but he cheats a little in order to get his rabbinic and philosophical authorities on the same page. The details of how he cheats—some of his prooftexts are straw men, and he ends up invoking a distinction between rational and irrational laws that he doesn't really believe—are less important than the fact that he feels compelled to do so. For the tension he identified is a genuine one.

If ethical action is a consequence of accepting "the yoke of the law," and the primary object of evaluation is the individual act, then the person who, against his own inclinations, bends himself to the commanded task is heroic. If ethical action is a matter of one's character, then that very same person will be just barely passable, like an alcoholic who is "on the wagon," at least for now.

One can see this tension still at work near the outset of Maimonides's great code of law, the *Mishneh Torah*. In its first volume, he codifies both *Hilchot De'ot*, "Laws of Moral Traits," and *Hilchot Teshuvah*, "Laws of Repentance." In *Hilchot De'ot* he briskly sketches an Aristotelian account of the virtues as a set of acquired habits whose ideal lies between two extremes. One case in which he unambiguously endorses straying from the middle path of classic virtue is instructive:

> There are some dispositions in regard to which it is forbidden merely to keep to the middle path. . . . Such a disposition is pride. The right way in this regard is not to be merely meek, but to be humble-minded and lowly of spirit to the utmost. And therefore was it said of Moses that he was "*exceedingly* meek," (Num. 12:3), not merely that he was "meek." Hence, our sages exhorted us, "Be exceedingly, exceedingly lowly of spirit" (Ethics of the Fathers 4:4). They also said that anyone who permits his heart to swell with haughtiness has denied the essential principal of our religion, as it is said, "And your heart will be proud, and you will forget the Lord your God" (Deut. 8:14).

This is very far from the virtuous person Aristotle called the "great-souled man" who thinks himself worthy of great things because he really is worthy of them. For Maimonides, it would seem impossible for such a man to understand that he is obliged to bow to the law and its giver, hence the deviation from the golden mean even by that greatest-souled of prophets, Moses.

Nonetheless, although the shadings are different, the overall picture of moral life given in *Hilchot De'ot* is an Aristotelian one. A good and happy human life is the natural result of the cultivation and exercise of the virtues, which is, more or less, equivalent to following the commandments of the Torah. Indeed, even the afterlife is a natural result of the highest of these virtues, those of the intellect. Given such a picture, it is almost as impossible to have a good, flourishing life without a good upbringing, parents, and education as it would be to cultivate a vegetable garden in permafrost. This makes the religious obligation to repent a bit of a problem. "Ought," as they say, "implies can."

IN *HILCHOT TESHUVAH*, Maimonides famously defines complete repentance as having been demonstrated when a person is faced with an opportunity to commit the same offense and refrains from doing so "because of his repentance rather than fear or failure." Since it is a commandment to repent, this is incumbent upon all Jews, but what if they lack the resources to pull this off?

In his discussion of repentance, Maimonides devotes an entire chapter to insisting that we have free will, but that sidesteps the problem. Aristotle argued that choosing virtue or vice was up to us. But he also thought such choices had a shelf life; there is a time when it is unfortunately too late to become a courageous or truthful person, just as it can be too late to begin training as a triathlete or a poet. How in such a system can repentance be obligatory? Yom Kippur, for instance, might seem like a good tool to rethink one's habits and reprioritize one's desires, but focusing on particular sins is really secondary to the vices that gave rise to them, and vices cannot be erased in a day.

One sees the strain between Maimonides's commitments to an ethics of character, on the one hand, and an ethics of obligation, on the other, when he writes about repentance in old age:

> If a person only repented in old age, at a time when he is
> no longer capable of doing what he had once done, this
> is not an excellent form of repentance, but he is counted
> as a penitent. Even if he transgressed his entire life and
> repented on the day of his death and died as a penitent, all
> of his sins are forgiven.

One can perhaps reconcile such a statement with the virtue ethics laid out in *Hilchot De'ot*, but it is also clear here that

Maimonides has reservations about someone whose repentance consists largely or entirely of regret. Indeed, what can such a verbal repentance even mean if it does not draw upon the kind of moral resources that MacIntyre enumerated, and does not issue in the kind of behavioral change that Maimonides set out as a criterion of success? One suspects that Maimonides would have been tempted to agree with Montaigne, who said that he saw "nothing of conscience" in deathbed repentance: "[C]hagrin and feebleness imprint on us a lax and snotty virtue."

But is this really fair? And would one want to live in a moral culture in which repentance was no longer a possibility for those who were badly raised, or fully formed, or near death? Perhaps what Maimonides and the Jewish tradition he is summarizing are suggesting is that if one does not have the resources to change one's desires, then God will provide them. Or, alternatively, that in insisting that repentance is always both obligatory and possible, that "the gates of repentance" reopen every year, the tradition itself provides the resources to "stop doing the things that you know are wrong," through the social instruments of religion, the community, and the law. But it does not guarantee that one will.

What then of Maimonides's virtue ethics? Perhaps his inconsistent—or at least tension-ridden—system in which our moral lives are described in terms of both virtues to cultivate and commandments to be obeyed is closer to our felt experience than either is alone. Moral thinking, it turns out, was always messy.

No Game for Old Men:
Baseball, Steroids,
and the Mitchell Report

KIKI CUYLER was a terrific right-fielder for the Pittsburgh Pirates and the Chicago Cubs in the 1920s and 30s, a Johnny Damon-type player with speed and extra-base power. In 1925 he hit .357 and led the National League in triples and runs scored. From 1926 through 1930, he led the league in stolen bases in every year but one. In the mid-30s, after an injury, Cuyler started to slow down. He played his last season with the Brooklyn Dodgers as a second-string outfielder, and was out of the majors by the age of forty.

A couple of years later, Cuyler's son was offered a spot on a minor-league team. According to Bill James, in his *Baseball Historical Abstract*, Kiki knew that his son was not good enough, and wanted to spare him the pain of finding out. "Look, son," he said, "I had to leave the major leagues because my legs have gone back on me, and that's why I'm through as a player. But I'll race you a hundred yards. If you beat me, I'll say it's all right to go ahead. If I beat you, you'll give it up." Kiki won by fifteen yards, going away.

Nowadays, to judge by former U.S. Senator George Mitchell's recently delivered 409-page *Report to the Commissioner of Baseball of an Independent Investigation Into the Illegal Use of Steroids and Other Performance-Enhancing Substances by Players in Major League Baseball*, a player like Kiki, and maybe even his son, would have other options.

Performance-enhancing drugs are most tempting to players at the margins of talent, health, and, perhaps most of all, age. A minor leaguer—especially one who is not a power hitter—can muscle up to get to the majors. A good pitcher can move into the superstar category by throwing a faster fastball. With the use of anabolic steroids, a great hitter can build extraordinary muscle mass, increase his endurance, and prolong his dominance. For older players, human-growth hormone (HGH) can speed the healing after an injury, help tired bodies bounce back from workouts, and prevent the muscle deterioration that comes with age.

In fact, aside from sudden changes in physique or increases in home runs and other "power" statistics, the easiest way to tell if a baseball player is, as they say, on the juice, is if his career does *not* describe an arc more or less like Kiki Cuyler's: peaking in the mid to late twenties, plateauing for a few years, and in decline by the mid to late thirties. A truly great player like Willie Mays might peak earlier and plateau for longer, but the shape of the curve is—not coincidentally—as inexorable as death.

Or at least it was until recently. Mays's first great year was 1954, when he was twenty-three. His last excellent year was thirteen years later in 1966. When, as a child, I saw him play at Candlestick Park in 1971, his legs, like Kiki Cuyler's, had "gone back" on him, and his play was quickly deteriorating.

As it happens, the modern-day player most comparable to Willie Mays is his godson Barry Bonds. But Bonds had the best offensive year of his or arguably anyone's career at the advanced age of thirty-six, hitting a staggering seventy-three home runs. Indeed, Bonds is unique in having played his five best years after the age of thirty-five, which is to say—again not coincidentally—after he is alleged to have begun taking anabolic steroids.

Senator Mitchell's report was commissioned by the corporation known as Major League Baseball, which happens to be a principal beneficiary of the rekindled public interest in the game induced by steroids-powered record-breaking. On those grounds alone, expectations for the report were not exactly high to begin with. Although Mitchell begins on a strong note—"there has been widespread illegal use of anabolic steroids and other performance-enhancing substances by players in Major League Baseball, in violation of federal law and baseball policy"—and although he and his team uncovered some striking new facts and allegations, the report was no surprise to anyone who had been paying attention over the last couple of decades.

Twenty years ago, in the *Washington Post*, the sports columnist Tom Boswell remarked of José Canseco, then a speedy young power-hitter with the Oakland A's, that he was the best example of a player "who has become great through steroids." By his own later account in *Juiced* (2005), Canseco was the Johnny Appleseed of anabolic steroids. In the late 80s, he introduced them to teammates, including Mark McGwire. "It was really no big deal," Canseco writes. "We would just slip away, get our syringes and vials, and head into the bathroom." A few years later, playing for the Texas Rangers, he was injecting Rafael Palmeiro, Juan Gonzalez, and Iván Rodriguez, each of whom improved significantly as a home-run hitter.

Other players learned of the good news from elsewhere. Around the same time, outfielder Lenny Dykstra of the Philadelphia Phillies was cheerily attributing his off-season addition of thirty-odd pounds of muscle to working with free weights and "really good vitamins." In 1996, Brady Anderson, a lead-off hitter for the Baltimore Orioles who had never managed more than twenty-one home runs in a season, suddenly hit fifty—a feat that Hank Aaron, Ted Williams, and Reggie Jackson never achieved.

Two years later, in the midst of Mark McGwire's spectacular 1998 duel with Sammy Sosa to break the season record of sixty-one home runs, a reporter noticed a bottle of andro-stenedione in McGwire's locker. "Andro" is a prohormone, which, while legal in baseball at the time, was designed, like anabolic steroids, to artificially raise the athlete's level of testosterone. An earlier version had been used by the big-shouldered East German Olympic women's teams of yore and was already banned in football and the Olympics.

The *New York Times* ran the story under the headline, "The News Is Out: Popeye Spikes His Spinach," though by then McGwire looked more like Bluto. He ended the season with seventy home runs, ten more than Babe Ruth had hit in 1927 and nine more than Roger Maris in 1961. Contemplating his achievement, McGwire famously remarked that he was "like, in awe of myself."

So was major-league baseball, which had been languishing after the disastrous strike-shortened season of 1994 and was now regaining its status as America's pastime. And so were others. According to the reporters Mark Fainaru-Wada and Lance Williams in *Game of Shadows* (2006), the certainty that McGwire was using much more than over-the-counter "andro" helped convince Barry Bonds to find a trainer who would supervise a serious steroids and weight-training regimen. Within three years, Bonds had broken McGwire's single-season record.

In the fall of 2000, interviewed on a nationally syndicated radio show, Jason Giambi of the Oakland A's spoke with a jocularity bordering on candor about his own massive physique and repeatedly referred to Barry Bonds, then in the first year of his great steroids-fueled run, as a "cartoon character." Major League Baseball was evidently not listening. In response to the increase in home runs that year, Commissioner Bud Selig requested an investigation into the manufacture and composition of baseballs. The investigative team took a trip to the Rawlings plant in Costa Rica and found that the cork centers of the balls were not being "juiced." Nobody asked whether the players were.

Others, however, were paying attention. In 2003, both Giambi and Bonds came under investigation for their patronage of the Bay Area Laboratory Cooperative (BALCO), which specialized in undetectable boutique steroids. The ongoing BALCO scandal, together with the debacle of congressional hearings in 2005 in which McGwire brokenly repeated that he would not "talk about the past," and Rafael Palmeiro defiantly insisted that he had never used steroids, only to test positive shortly thereafter, led in turn to the commissioning of Mitchell's report.

The report goes over this and a great deal more public information. None of it is news: the pharmacological genie has long been out of the bottle, and the use of steroids in other sports, most prominently track-and-field and cycling, is well known. Why should baseball be any different? As a minor leaguer told the writer Will Carroll, "if shooting bull piss was going to get me ten more home runs, fine." No amount of congressional harrumphing, "Say-it-ain't-so, Joe" pleas from broken-hearted youngsters, or reports of awful side effects (shrunken testicles, a literally inflated head, uncontrollable rage, severe depression, immunosuppression, cancer) will change this.

Still, the report is valuable for the wealth and specificity of its detail. This is largely due to the cooperation of Kirk Radomski, a former New York Mets batboy and clubhouse employee, and his customer Brian McNamee, formerly a strength coach for the Toronto Blue Jays and the New York Yankees. Radomski signed a plea agreement with the U.S. Attorney's office in which he admitted to selling anabolic steroids, HGH, and amphetamines to dozens of major-league players from 1995 through 2005. McNamee signed a similar agreement. Both face further charges if they can be shown to have lied to investigators.

What Radomski and McNamee's testimony revealed was not an organized conspiracy but more like a high school with rampant drug use. There were overlapping groups of incompetent dealers and giddy users exchanging drugs, information, and misinformation. Steroids and syringes were delivered by Federal Express to players at the clubhouse, kept in their lockers, and used in the bathrooms. Private "trainers" had wide access to the clubhouse.

All this was abetted by very lax discipline on the part of Major League Baseball—understandable enough, since, at least in the short term, it profited from the practice. Team officials privately discussed which players they thought were on steroids. Thus, in notes from a Los Angeles Dodgers meeting reproduced by Mitchell, the talk came around to Paul Lo Duca: "Got off the steroids . . . took away a lot [of] hard line drives." This was said more in sorrow over the lost hits than in anger over illegal doping. Meanwhile, the Players Association strenuously resisted testing for drugs and seems to have tipped off its members to impending tests. Mitchell notes elsewhere that teams failing to report information about their players' use of banned substances were liable to a two million dollar fine. None has ever been assessed.

Of course, the biggest headlines about the report have concerned Roger Clemens, who was trained by Brian McNamee. As with Bonds, Clemens's career path had described a trajectory similar to that of previous great players—until the "decline phase" of middle age, when suddenly it shot up like a rocket. McNamee asserted that he administered a variety of steroids and, for a while, HGH to Clemens. But in a series of increasingly vociferous and not entirely plausible staged events designed to protect his reputation as the greatest pitcher of his generation, Clemens has denied taking steroids. The truth is that Roger Clemens *is* the greatest pitcher of his generation—albeit someone who, just like the greatest hitter of his generation, does appear to have called on artificial aids in order to extend his run.

Seeing Bud Selig piously endorse before Congress the findings and recommendations of the Mitchell report, one was inevitably reminded of the scene in *Casablanca* in which Captain Renault announces he is "shocked, shocked" to discover gambling going on even as he collects his winnings. One question is just how long Major-League Baseball can continue to cash in. But a more interesting question, at least for the serious fan as spring training begins, is what all this means for our enjoyment of the game.

W.H. Auden has some nice lines about watching someone who has found an activity at which he excels:

> You need not see what someone is doing
> to know if it is his vocation,
> you have only to watch his eyes:
> a cook mixing a sauce, a surgeon
> making a primary incision,
> a clerk completing a bill of lading,
> wear the same rapt expression,
> forgetting themselves in a function.
> How beautiful it is,
> that eye-on-the-object look.

Watching Barry Bonds at bat during his spectacular steroids-fueled run was like that. One saw what it really meant to "keep your eye on the ball." He stood at the plate, massive, poised, and discerning, with that eye-on-the-object look: ready to hit anything hittable but willing to walk if the pitch was even minimally off the plate. In 2004, Bonds got on base better than sixty percent of the time, breaking Ted Williams's record when he hit .406 and walked 147 times in 1941.

There is a story about Williams at bat toward the end of his career. With each pitch, the young catcher for the opposing team complains to the umpire: "You call that a ball?" After the third such complaint, the umpire replies: "Young man, when your pitcher throws a strike, Mr. Williams will let you know." Watching Bonds was like that, too, or at least as close as those of us too young to have seen Williams will ever get to seeing a baseball player hit with seemingly effortless precision and power. He was both rapt and ready, forgetting himself in the function of hitting. This is the beauty to be had in sports: to see a human being perfectly adapt his body to the arbitrary, almost impossible requirements of a game in unrehearsed real time.

But if that is so, why should I, as a fan, resent Bonds for, at great cost to his own body and reputation, affording me the experience of such beauty? To return to the *New York Times*'s favorite literary allusion, why should we cheer Popeye but boo Barry? Or, perhaps closer to home, why do we root for Joe Hardy in the musical comedy *Damn Yankees* when he makes a Faustian bargain to exchange his broken-down, middle-aged body for that of a brilliant young ballplayer? In fact the case for Bonds is stronger, since, no matter what "performance-enhancing" drugs were involved, no one else in major-league baseball could have become the hitter he became.

In short, what is wrong with the libertarian argument to which Bonds himself has sometimes gestured? What is wrong with just letting "the show," as players call the major leagues, be a show—and not worrying about what goes on backstage?

One way to see the weakness of this argument is by means of a thought experiment. Last spring, in a spectacular lapse of taste and good judgment, ESPN began airing a reality television show on Bonds's pursuit of Hank Aaron's all-time home-run record. Called *Bonds on Bonds*, the show, which was eventually canceled, gave supposed behind-the-scenes glimpses into his preparations for the game. Imagine if this had included the carefully calibrated and charted ministrations of Bonds's personal trainer Greg Anderson. If it is a Monday, Wednesday, or Friday, then an HGH belly-button shot. On Mondays and Wednesdays, BALCO's undetectable designer drug "The Clear" is placed under the tongue. On Tuesdays, "The Cream" is massaged onto the elbow. The three-week cycle would end with a climactic Clomid pill, and then viewers could be treated to the suspense of wondering whether Bonds's power would drop during the off-week before the next cycle began.

The point is that it is important to us that great athletes push the limits of human achievement. But it has to be *human* achievement. Seeing Bonds in batting practice or on the weight machines in his pre-steroid days might have been boring, but at least these exercises would have had an internal relationship to the athletic virtues of strength, speed, and coordination that he demonstrated on the field. Performance-enhancing drugs are literally, even sickeningly, external.

It is not as if someone other than Mark McGwire hit seventy home runs in 1998; but it is not quite as if the middle-aged McGwire did, either. He may have intuited something like this in his apparently fatuous remark that he was "in awe" of himself. Awe is not really an attitude one can feel toward oneself. Perhaps he was in awe of the body he had become.

We have a kind of reverse-Frankenstein problem: not "has the monster become human," but "has the human become monstrous"? And are we as interested in seeing these players throw fastballs and hit home runs once we know that they are monsters or virtual post-humans? This is a particular problem in baseball, where numbers—60, 61, .406—stand for iconic achievements and serve as landmarks in the history and tradition of the game. Can the tradition hold together if the numbers change with the speed of pharmaceutical advances?

The steroids scandal is unique in the history of baseball. It involves no cheating on the field; no spitballs, no fixing of games. It may have been so widespread that it did not even upset the overall competitive balance of play. Finally, unlike the cocaine scandals of the 80s, it most certainly did not result in worse play on the field. Nonetheless, if the loosely Aristotelian argument I have been suggesting is correct, this scandal could kill or at least radically transform our understanding and appreciation of what baseball, and sport more generally, is. Indeed, it may already have happened.

When Willie Mays was a teenager he played on a factory team in Alabama with his father, who was called Kitty Kat because of his grace in the field. Kitty Kat was in his mid-thirties and Willie was sixteen. In his autobiography, Mays described the last time they played together. A batter hit a sinking liner to left center:

> I heard my father say "all right, all right, let me take it." But then I knew that the ball was sinking and he was too far back, and I saw that if I cut in front of him, I could handle it, so I did and caught it off the grasstops.

A. Bartlett Giamatti, the late commissioner of baseball, who, unlike Bud Selig, revered baseball and could turn a phrase, spoke of the game as an arcadia in which the play was "graceful, energetic, and free in the order and law of a green field." As a Renaissance scholar, Giamatti would also have known that there is death, or at least a hint of it, even in arcadia. This is a lesson that, if it is not too late, baseball should learn and teach its players. Like Kiki Cuyler, Willie Mays, Sr., knew it. He never played again.

Light Reading

IN MICHAEL CHABON'S *Telegraph Avenue*, Archy Stallings carries around a paperback copy of Marcus Aurelius's *Meditations* "that he must have read ninety-three times." Archy, a jazz musician, wayward husband, and almost-father who sells vinyl records in Oakland, is more lovable screw-up than Stoic, and we never do learn exactly what he treasures in the *Meditations*, but Stoicism has been making a comeback of late.

Back in 1998, around when Chabon's novel is set, the hero of Tom Wolfe's *A Man in Full* discovers Epictetus in prison and comes out preaching the good word of *apatheia*, or freedom from passion. "We ought not spend our feelings on things beyond our power," Epictetus said, which is good advice when possible, especially for those obsessed with the things Tom Wolfe's characters tend to be obsessed with (money, prestige, excellent trapezius muscles). A few years later, William Irvine wrote a pretty good self-help book called *A Guide to the Good Life: The Ancient Art of Stoic Joy*. (Irvine, a professional philosopher, rather charmingly admitted that he first learned of Stoic ethics from Wolfe's novel.) Down at the deep end of the philosophical pool,

Martha Nussbaum has elaborated an interesting Neo-Stoic theory of emotions.

More recently, classicist Philip Freeman has repackaged some of Cicero's political insights in a little book entitled *How to Run a Country: An Ancient Guide for Modern Leaders*, and Seneca is the philosophical hero of Nassim Nicholas Taleb's best-selling *Antifragile: Things That Gain from Disorder*, although as far as I can tell the Roman philosopher is never quite quoted directly. "My idea of the modern Stoic sage," the *Black Swan* guru of financial pessimism says, "is *someone who transforms fear into prudence, pain into information, mistakes into initation and desire into undertaking.*" Italics notwithstanding, this is not always possible. The phrase "pain into information" reminds me of a moment early on in *Catch-22*, when Captain Yossarian's lover tells him that God created pain as a useful warning system. "Why couldn't he have used a doorbell, instead?" he asks. Maybe if Yossarian had carried Marcus Aurelius around he would know that neither pain nor doorbells are evils in and of themselves but only insofar as we regard them as such, and *this* is always in our power. Then again, maybe not.

Among Jewish philosophers, the Stoic ideal of "living in agreement with nature" comes out most clearly and deeply in Spinoza, who taught that the only freedom was in recognizing necessity. I was about to teach a Spinoza seminar when I realized that the ideals of Stoicism were not just impossibly difficult but false to human experience, or at any rate false to mine. I was in the Pediatric Intensive Care Unit of the Rainbow Babies & Children's Hospital sitting by the crib of my newborn daughter Bayla, who had just returned from what was—thank God—successful heart surgery. What I realized suddenly, viscerally, was that the ideal of being emotionally impervious, of "not spending feelings" on matters beyond my power, or of turning pain into information, wasn't just impossible, it wasn't desirable. Who would aspire to that?

TALES OF STOIC HEROISM are often impressive, especially when they are about personal heroism. Seneca tells of a certain Julius Canus who got up from a chess game and went to his execution discussing philosophy with as much tranquility as his near-contemporary Rabbi Akiva discussed the Shema with his disciples as he was being tortured to death. But who would want to be so anti-fragile when it comes to one's loved ones?

To aspire to an inhuman ideal was not unique to the Stoics; it may be a permanent temptation of philosophy. This semester I am teaching Maimonides, and I hope that we get to the magnificent end of the *Guide of the Perplexed*, in which he describes the four types of human perfection, "according to the ancient and modern philosophers." The first is perfection of goods or wealth. This, Maimonides, says, is plainly the lowest kind of perfection, because "if such a person were to look at himself he would discover that all this is outside him," and he could lose it all in a moment. The second kind of perfection is physical, which may be more intrinsic to the person, but only insofar as he is an animal—and not a particularly impressive one either. After all, Maimonides says, the strongest man is no match for a good mule, let alone a lion.

The third kind of perfection is that of moral virtue or character, which, Maimonides admits, reaches deeper. But if you were on a desert island, you would have no need of the virtues. "It is only with regard to others that man needs them and receives any benefit from them." This leaves us, or at least Maimonides, with the one and final human perfection: intellect.

Consider each of the three preceding types of perfection, and you will discover that they belong to others . . . or to you and others at the same time. This last perfection, however, belongs to yourself exclusively, and no one else has any share in it: "They will be yours alone, others will have no part with you." (Proverbs 5:17)

You, and only you, know what you know, and you would still know it on a desert island (or in the afterlife).

This also leaves Maimonides with a classic problem: Why spend any time at all on others when you could just spend all your time thinking? His answer, which ends the *Guide*, is justly famous: "the perfection of man is . . . achieved by him who has attained comprehension of God . . . and knows how God provides for His creatures . . . and grasping this aims in his own conduct at mercy, justice and righteousness, so as to imitate God." Just as God does not merely think the universe but, in His perfection, somehow turns, or overflows, toward it, and cares for it, so too the perfect human being turns toward his fellow creatures.

But is this enough? I doubt it.

Maimonides' God is precisely one who does not depend in any way on the world, though the world depends on Him. That works for an omnipotent God, but not for us. The care we have for another person isn't care at all if we are not dependent, vulnerable, and susceptible to pain that cannot be turned into information. The moral life is not an act of Neoplatonic noblesse oblige, as Maimonides would have it. Nor is it a Stoic recognition of inevitable human fragility.

According to Cicero, when Anaxagoras was told of his son's death, he replied "I was already aware that I had begotten a mortal."—But not, apparently, that he was one as well.

The Digression:
My Father and His Books

A DOCTOR WALKS into the examination room and tells his patient that the drugs aren't working and there isn't anything else to try.

> *Doctor:* You'll be taken off all medication and restricted to a diet of flapjacks and flounders.
>
> *Patient:* [*With hope*] Is that some kind of special diet?
>
> *Doctor:* No—just the only food thin enough for the nurse to slide under your door.

My father, David Socher, *alav ha-shalom* (or, as he pronounced it in his LA-Ashkenazi accent, *olive ha-sholom*—though no one ever pronounces *that* peace upon himself), loved that joke. Five years ago, when the oncologist uttered the word "hospice" and fled the room, my dad turned to me and my mother and said, "Well . . . flapjacks and flounders."

The last three months had been a sudden, long fall. I had read Homer with my son Coby in the summer before tenth grade, and during my father's illness I sometimes thought of what Hephaestus said about Zeus hurling him down from the heavens: "All day long I fell." Of course, he was Zeus' son and it was my father who was falling, falling.

I asked him if there was anything he felt was left unfinished or that he wanted to do. It felt trite and unlike us but also important to ask. He was weak and gray from the chemo, but also uncharacteristically nervous, jiggling his legs up and down like a runner before a race. "Well," he said, "I can't remember which part of the dialogue in the *Theaetetus* is the part that the Plato guys call 'The Digression.'"

MY FATHER'S MIND caught fire in 1960. In an Intro to Philosophy course at San Fernando Valley State, Donald Henze read a passage aloud from the first chapter of Bertrand Russell's *The Problems of Philosophy*:

> [I]f we take any common object of the sort that is supposed to be known by the senses, what the senses *immediately* tell us is not the truth about the object as it is apart from us . . . what we directly see and feel is merely "appearance," which we believe to be a sign of some "reality" behind. But if the reality is not what appears, have we any means of knowing whether there is any reality at all?

Then Henze paused a beat and said "kind of spooky, huh?" and my dad was hooked. Although he didn't end up getting a PhD and never worked as an academic philosopher, it is almost impossible for me to imagine what he was like before then.

My mother moved this summer, and I've been packing up my father's books: most of the classics of Western philosophy, those great Doubleday Anchor paperbacks of the 1950s and 1960s, the little Fontana Modern Masters books from the 70s, the works of Wittgenstein, commentaries on Wittgenstein, Wittgensteinian commentaries on others, virtually all of the must-reads of twentieth-century analytic philosophy, multiple copies of the little Dover Thrift Editions he loved to teach from (*The Hound of the Baskervilles, Flatland*)—many of them with his notes, both discriminating and indiscriminate.

My father was not easy on his books. He often wrote his name across the outer edge of their pages along with the date of purchase, so that you separated and re-formed the letters as you opened and closed them. (As a yeshiva student, I worried that this made them forbidden to read on Shabbos.) He read his books in the bath, kept them on the floor of his car, set hot coffee cups on them, jotted cryptic notes on their pages. Sometimes a title page or back cover was just the handiest piece of paper (in *Aesthetics: An Introduction* by Ruth L. Saw he wrote "Loan Officer" and a number in the 818 area code).

Among the deeply familiar books (the furniture of my childhood) I found while sorting and packing were two identical paperback copies of Santayana's little book *Three Philosophical Poets*. One copy was his mother's—my Nana's—copy, probably from when she went back to school in the 1950s. On the inside cover of the copy he'd later bought himself he wrote "p. 19: 'It is always the fleeting moment in which we live.'" Of course, most of his annotations don't deliver that kind of retrospective punch. A yellow Post-it in David Roochnik's *Of Art and Wisdom: Plato's Understanding of Techne* reads:

Sacajawea was born in 1787 AD.

Socrates was executed in 399 BC.

∴ [a logical symbol for "therefore"] Sacajawea and Socrates never had lunch.

My guess is that this was a note about the logical function of time in certain arguments—what kind of necessity was involved in that "therefore." Also, my dad was a wise guy.

His dog-eared copy of Timothy Chappell's annotated translation of Plato's *Theaetetus* is heavily marked up. On page nine, he's jotted down a list of those "Plato guys": Cornford, Bostic, Burnyeat, McDowell, Sosa, Sedley, . . . [indecipherable]. It's hard not to make each surviving trace of one's dead parent a relic, to imagine that my father is himself scattered among these hundreds of books, piled on the floor of his empty house.

When I was about fifteen, he briefly tried to become an insurance salesman. I don't know how long this lasted and I'm fairly sure that he never sold a policy, but there was some drama around a visit from two of his new colleagues at Prudential. Not only did the house need to be (relatively) neat, but my father was worried that the number of books, magazines, and journals in the living room might not hit the right note. We packed a few boxes and put them in the garage. When the insurance salesmen arrived, my dad got some beers out and the three of them stood around making awkward chit-chat. "Wow," they kept saying as they stared at all the remaining books, the casual untidiness of our living room, my mother's tomato plants in the front yard, "this sure is California living."

WHEN WE GOT HOME from the hospital, my father was too weak to read, but the next day, or maybe the day after that, I brought the *Theaetetus* over. Plato frames the dialogue as a record of conversations that took place decades earlier and are being read as Theaetetus is dying after the battle of Corinth. I don't know whether this was in the back of my father's mind (or at the front of it) in that moment in the oncologist's office. Before he was diagnosed, he had been writing his own somewhat jokey parallel dialogue in which a dying Theaetetus reassesses Socrates' arguments about the nature of knowledge ("Socrates has loaded the dice, if I may say so, Imendides"). So he might have been wondering if he had time to finish his dialogue when he asked about "The Digression."

That digression begins at line 172c1. Socrates says that philosophers tend to look awkward and ridiculous in courts of law, civic assemblies, committee meetings, and parties. They are like Thales, who fell in a well while gazing at the heavens, much to the amusement of a Thracian girl. However, Socrates soon shows that when unphilosophical men who excel in such settings are "dragged upwards" into discussions of what really matters, they find themselves looking ridiculous. Then Socrates pushes a little harder. Suppose, he says, that we tell such men that the "region which is untainted by evils will not receive them even when they die," for they have been unconcerned with the eternal patterns of goodness while they lived. Maybe my father had been trying to remember this line when he asked his question. It was certainly a hard sentence to read to him in the fleeting moment.

Then again, my father was at the very end of a good, modest, thoughtful life and was, in any case, untempted by Plato's heaven. On the title page of McDowell's translation of the *Theaetetus*, which I have just reopened, I wrote "p. 54: Dad-Digression-Flapjacks-Heaven."

Kaddish and Eternity

And so, if following Plato, we wish to give things their right names, let us say that God is eternal, but the world is everlasting.
—Boethius, *The Consolation of Philosophy*, Book V

We're all gonna be here forever/So Momma don't you make such a stir/Just put down that camera/And come on and join up/The last of the family reserve.
—Lyle Lovett, "Family Reserve," *Joshua Judges Ruth* (1992)

ONCE, WHEN I WAS eleven or twelve, my mother said "When I die, I expect to go to heaven and I expect to see my daddy there." I don't know exactly what occasioned her statement of metaphysical confidence at that particular moment, standing in the dining room. My grandfather had been dead for at least a decade, but she still missed him, regretted the sad circumstances of his final days, and never shied from bold declarations. "Well," said my father, "how old will you be and how old will he be?"

Such questions are almost as venerable as the hopes for a world to come that they challenge, but, of course, I didn't know that at the time and my father's response startled me. I had neither been taught nor pondered any particular doctrine of eternal life, but it hadn't occurred to me that the idea might be not just unlikely, but difficult to make any sense of at all. My father's question came back to me when I recited the Mourner's Kaddish for him a few years ago. I did not find the prayer consoling, but then it was not written to console, and famously does not mention death or promise an afterlife. The Kaddish began sometime in the early rabbinic period as what historians of liturgy call a "doxology," a statement of belief that, in this case, was recited, at least at first, primarily after a sermon.

The sonorous Aramaic chant of the Kaddish is familiar, but the words are worthy of close attention, in part because they do suggest a theological notion of eternity, though, strikingly, not one that is humanly attainable. The prayer begins

> Magnified and sanctified may His great name be in the
> world which He created by His will. May He establish
> His kingdom in your lifetime and in your days and in the
> lifetime of all the house of Israel, swiftly and soon. And
> say: Amen.

What is devoutly wished for here is a theological-political achievement—the establishment of His kingdom—within time: "in your lifetime . . . and in the lifetime of all the house of Israel." It is at this point that the entire congregation responds with its key declaration:

> May his great name be praised forever and all time.

The phrase Jonathan Sacks translates here as "forever and all time," and others have translated as "forever and ever," is *lealam uleolomei almaia*. Both are attempts to convey the sense of the prayer's three-fold intensification of the Aramaic form of the Hebrew word *olam*, which in the Bible was often used to mean permanent or indefinite or everlasting existence, though by the time of the Kaddish's composition it had also come to denote the world or universe. The content of the congregation's response, then, is not so much one of direct praise but rather the hope that such human praise will continue forever and ever. The classical Hebrew analogue to this Aramaic phrase is *barukh shem kevod malchuto le-olam va-ed*, "blessed be the name of his glorious kingship (or kingdom) forever and ever," which was originally employed in response to the High Priest's invocation of God's ineffable name.

The reader's reply to the congregation's expression of hope that God's name be praised forever reads not only as an immediate attempt to fulfill it, but also as a metaphysical clarification or caveat:

> Blessed and praised, glorified and exalted, raised and honored, uplifted and lauded be the name of the Holy One, blessed be He, [who is] beyond any blessings and hymns, praises and consolations which may be uttered in the world. And say Amen.

There are, it seems, two distinctions being made here. The first is between "the name of the Holy One Blessed Be He,"—itself repeatedly alluded to but strikingly never actually uttered in the prayer—and the divine bearer of that name, who is conventionally described as "the Holy One Blessed Be He," but only directly referred to with the simple third-person pronoun. The second, more implicit, distinction is between the kind of eternity that can be predicated of a name or its praise, even the great name, and that which can be predicated of the bearer of that name. The first kind of eternity is, even if it continues forever, within time; it consists in an endless series of utterances "in the world." The assertion that the bearer of the divine name is beyond all such praise suggests a different, perhaps more Platonic, sort of eternity.

THE OR ZARUA, a thirteenth-century work by the Ashkenazi Pietist Isaac ben Moshe of Vienna, is apparently the first to describe the custom of reciting the *Kaddish Yatom*, the "Orphan's Kaddish," which was recited by an orphan at the end of the Sabbath. This was a key moment in the historical process of turning the Kaddish into a prayer of mourning. That the Kaddish should have become such a prayer despite its failure to mention death, or the afterlife, or to offer any words of consolation (unlike, for instance, medieval Catholic prayers for the dead) is famously surprising and an issue to which I shall return, but it is not entirely so.

There is a well-established rabbinic practice of affirming *tzidduk hadin*, the justice of the (divine) decree, in the face of tragedy. Hence, the still-current practice of saying *barukh dayan ha-emet* upon hearing of someone's passing. I have heard this taken—and even offered—as an expression of consolation, but what it actually means is "Blessed is the true Judge," that is the Judge is blessed even, or particularly, at a moment when the bereaved might be tempted to curse Him, or deny that His judgment is true, or even that there is a divine judge at all. In fact, the most powerful expression of unbelief in the rabbinic tradition is *leit din ve-leit dayan*, "there is no judgment and there is no judge." The Kaddish's determination that God be praised forever, in the context of mourning, is an affirmation that there is, and will always be, a judge.

At least one reason for choosing the Kaddish to express faith in God's judgment is a strange story about the great second-century Rabbi Akiva, which appears in an odd early medieval compilation of rabbinic legends called the *Alphabet of Rabbi Akiva*, and is retold in the *Or Zarua* and elsewhere. In this story, Rabbi Akiva is walking in a cemetery and meets a naked man carrying an impossibly heavy burden of wood and hurrying "like a horse." Rabbi Akiva, thinking that he is speaking to a live human being, asks if there is any way he can relieve him of his duties. But it turns out that the man is, in fact, dead and suffering the punishments of hell (Gehenna) for his sins as a tax collector. How can he be relieved of his torments? Only if his abandoned son comes before a congregation, says *barkhu et adonai ha-mevorakh* ("let us bless God Who is blessed") and is answered with *yehe shmei rabba mevorakh* ("may his great name be blessed"). With some difficulty, Rabbi Akiva manages to make this happen. This, says the *Or Zarua*, is the precedent for an orphan to recite Kaddish.

Several scholars have noted the medieval Christian context and flavor of the idea that prayer can relieve the purgatorial suffering of our loved ones. This is important, but I want to return here to the Kaddish's sense of eternity and what strikes me as a deep philosophical irony in choosing this, of all prayers, as the vehicle for easing our loved ones' afterlife. To return to the distinctions which I identified in the Kaddish: God is not to be identified with his name, and it is only his name, a word in mortal human mouths and documents, which can be praised forever and ever. It will, in short, be endlessly praised if we never stop praising it. But God is, the Kaddish asserts, untouched by such praise: "He is beyond all blessings and hymns, praises and consolations which may be uttered in the world."

That is, the prayer itself seems to agree with Boethius, among others, in distinguishing between the everlastingness which can characterize the world and its contents, and eternity as a kind of timelessness, which is beyond the world. The mystery and power of "the great Name," at least here, would seem to be that it is a part of this world while managing to refer to that which is beyond it.

One could map these rabbinic thoughts about God, eternity, and time more systematically onto this or that philosophical theory. And the evident importance given to—and perhaps philosophical puzzlement over—the this-worldly name of an unworldly and timeless being in the text of the Kaddish is philosophically suggestive. But I think that, here and elsewhere, it would do violence to rabbinic thinking to over-systematize it.

Let us end, rather, with the irony that nothing in the text of the Kaddish itself suggests that anything in the world, including us, or any temporal successors we may have after our death, can escape into a timeless afterlife. Indeed, such timelessness would appear to be, at least according to the Kaddish, an exclusive property of God.

Acknowledgments

Although I have tinkered with most of the essays in this collection, I am indebted to each of the editors who first commissioned and edited them, and I thank them and their publications for permission to republish the essays in revised form here.

I owe a particular debt of gratitude to the two great editors for whom the earliest of these pieces were written, Alan Jenkins at the *Times Literary Supplement* (*TLS*) and Neal Kozodoy at *Commentary Magazine*. Alan published my essays on Vladimir Nabokov's *Pale Fire* and Walter Benjamin's (or, rather, Mount Sinai's) remarkable rocks (both under different titles, in the July 1, 2005, and March 7, 2008, editions, respectively). Neal published my review of Cynthia Ozick's *Dictation* (*Commentary*, September, 2008) and my piece on Senator Mitchell's report on steroids in baseball (March, 2008). Years later, he also published "Hello, I Must Be Going," in *Mosaic Magazine* (May, 2014). John Podhoretz, Neal's successor at *Commentary*, commissioned my long essay on the case of Oberlin College v. Gibson's Bakery, which was published (and went viral, or at least as viral as a professor's 8,000-word lamentation can go) under John's funny Whitmanesque title "Oh Oberlin, My Oberlin!" (October, 2019).

Most of the other essays were first published in the *Jewish Review of Books*, and I thank my editorial colleagues Allan Arkush, Phil Getz, and Amy Newman Smith for perceptive and challenging comments on early drafts of these pieces. Allan also commissioned the "Nonsense is Nonsense" piece for *AJS Perspectives* (Fall 2006) before we founded the JRB. The late Elliott Horowitz commissioned my essay on Solomon Schechter for a special issue of the venerable *Jewish Quarterly Review* (Spring 2016), and my friend Yitzhak Melamed asked for the little essay on the Mourner's Kaddish, which closes both this volume and Melamed's *Eternity: A History* (Oxford University Press, 2016).

My son Dani Socher and former JRB Associate Editor Michal Leibowitz both read and commented on a penultimate version of this collection (I now find myself wondering whether I took enough of their perceptive comments to heart). This was before I handed over the long-promised manuscript to the incomparable—and incomparably patient—Paul Dry. I thank Paul for some great conversations and innumerable excellent comments; Julia Sippel's line-edits and queries were tactful, timely, and incisive, all that I could ask for.

Acharon, Acharon Chaviv, as Rashi once said (meaning, roughly, the last mentioned is the most beloved), I thank my wife Shoshana without whom . . .

Abraham Socher is the editor of the *Jewish Review of Books*, which he founded, and a professor emeritus of Jewish Studies and Religion at Oberlin College. His recent edition of the *Autobiography of Solomon Maimon* (Princeton University Press) was a finalist for a National Jewish Book Award. Socher lives with his family in Beachwood, Ohio.